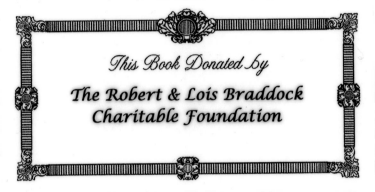

NO COMPROMISE

The Story of Harvey Milk

CIVIL RIGHTS LEADERS

Ella Baker

W. E. B. Du Bois

Harvey Milk

A. Philip Randolph

Bayard Rustin

Roy Wilkins

NO COMPROMISE

The Story of Harvey Milk

David Aretha

MORGAN
REYNOLDS
PUBLISHING

Greensboro, North Carolina

No Compromise : The Story of Harvey Milk

Copyright © 2010 Morgan Reynolds Publishing

Library of Congress Cataloging-in-Publication Data

Aretha, David.
  No compromise : the story of Harvey Milk / by David Aretha. -- 1st ed.
    p. cm.
  Includes bibliographical references and index.
  ISBN 978-1-59935-129-2 (alk. paper)
  1. Milk, Harvey--Juvenile literature. 2. Politicians--California--San Francisco--Biography--Juvenile literature. 3. Gay politicians--California--San Francisco--Biography--Juvenile literature. 4. San Francisco (Calif.)--Politics and government--20th century--Juvenile literature. I. Title.
  F869.S353M545 2009
  979.4'61053092--dc22
  [B]

                                        2009025708

Printed in the United States of America
First edition

CONTENTS

"WAKE UP, AMERICA"

1

On a hot June day in San Francisco, during the largest Gay Freedom Day Parade the city had ever seen, people wanted to kill Harvey Milk. As one postcard to Milk declared, "You get the first bullet the minute you stand at the microphone."

Tensions between homosexuals and those opposed to the gay rights movement had reached a high pitch by June 25, 1978. Milk, the outspoken voice of the gay community, was a lightning rod for bigotry. In 1977, he had been elected as a city supervisor in San Francisco, making him one of the first openly gay Americans elected to public office in a major U.S. city. He now was using his position to fight for the rights of gays, lesbians, and other oppressed minorities. He had entered the battle with his typical brash courage.

In 1978 Milk, and the rest of the gay/lesbian community, was most concerned about Proposition 6. The brainchild of California senator John Briggs, Prop 6—if passed by voters in November 1978—would force California school systems to fire gay and lesbian teachers. Male school kids, Briggs insisted, risked sexual molestation from gay teachers. The statistics on child abuse did not support this claim. Nevertheless, it looked as though most voters were buying into the myth. That summer, polls showed that two-thirds of Californians were ready to vote for Proposition 6.

Harvey Milk

(Courtesy of Dan Nicoletta)

Milk vociferously denounced Prop 6, as well as John Briggs and singer and former beauty pageant contestant, Anita Bryant, who was the spokesperson for Save Our Children. That organization was based on "Christian beliefs regarding the sinfulness of homosexuality and the perceived threat of homosexual recruitment of children and child molestation." Over the previous year, Save Our Children had been the driving force behind successful movements to repeal anti-discrimination ordinances in several U.S. cities. Because Milk spoke out for gay rights and attacked the anti-gay initiatives, he was despised by many supporters of the anti-gay movement. In the days before the Gay Freedom Day Parade, his life had been threatened several times.

Euphoria swept over much of San Francisco that Sunday afternoon. Gays, lesbians, and supporters—300,000 strong—celebrated both their pride and their determination to fight for equal rights. A marching band led the way, and those from out of town raised signs declaring where they were from. "I'm from Woodmere, N.Y.," Milk's sign announced.

Wearing a T-shirt and lei, Milk sat up on the backseat of a convertible, waving to the crowd. A man of great mood swings, he now beamed brightly, buoyed by the festive crowd. City officials, concerned for his life, had offered Milk police protection. But he refused. He wanted to be out in the open, both figuratively and literally.

Finally, Milk reached the microphone, where the postcard had predicted he'd be assassinated. Seemingly fearless, Milk addressed the massive crowd.

"My name is Harvey Milk—and I want to recruit you," he declared. "I want to recruit you for the fight to preserve democracy from the John Briggs and Anita Bryant who are trying to constitutionalize bigotry."

Energized by the crowd, Milk continued with his fiery speech. He said that gays were not going to be oppressed by society the

In this June 26, 1978, file photo, San Francisco supervisor Harvey Milk is seen in San Francisco's seventh annual Gay Freedom Day parade. (*Courtesy of AP Images*)

way German homosexuals were by the Nazi regime during World War II.

"I ask my gay sisters and brothers to make the commitment to fight . . . ," he said. "Gay people, we will not win our rights by staying quietly in our closets. . . . We are coming out. We are coming out to fight the lies, the myths, the distortions. We are coming out to tell the truths about gays, for I am tired of the conspiracy of silence, so I'm going to talk about it. And I want you to talk about it. You must come out."

For Milk, the gloves were off. Not even the president was off-limits.

"Jimmy Carter," he said, "you talk about human rights. You want to be the world's leader for human rights. There are 15 to 20 million gay people in this nation. When are you going to talk about their rights?"

The crowd shouted cries of support. Rarely, if ever, had they heard a gay man use such forceful words. Milk called for a march on Washington, similar to the famous civil rights march in 1963 that demanded equal rights for black Americans. He alluded to Martin Luther King's "I Have a Dream" speech:

"I call upon all minorities and especially the millions of lesbians and gay men to wake up from their dreams, to gather in Washington and tell Jimmy Carter and their nation: Wake up. Wake up, America. No more racism. No more sexism. No more ageism. No more hatred. No more . . ."

Milk offered a reminder to John Briggs, Anita Bryant, and "the bigots." The Statue of Liberty, he said, offers this message: "Give me your tired, your poor, your huddled masses yearning to be free." The Declaration of Independence, he said, states: "All men are created equal, and they are endowed with certain inalienable rights." And the national anthem, he said, states: "Oh, say does that star-spangled banner yet wave o'er the land of the free."

"For Mr. Briggs and Ms. Bryant . . . and all the bigots out there: That's what America is. No matter how hard you try, you cannot erase those words from the Declaration of Independence. No matter how hard you try, you cannot chip those words off the base of the Statue of Liberty. And no matter how hard you try, you cannot sing the 'Star-Spangled Banner' without those words. That's what America is," Milk declared. "Love it or leave it."

When he was done, Milk—always looking for ways to maximize publicity for the movement—handed out copies of his speech to every reporter he could find.

No one took a shot at Harvey Milk that day. But ominously, within the sea of humanity, a fellow member of the San Francisco Board of Supervisors grumbled to himself. Dan White, a clean-cut "All-American" guy, complained to reporters about the immoral dress of those at the parade.

Dan White didn't like gays, and he would grow to despise Harvey Milk. In five months and two days, he would fire five bullets into Milk's body, including two to the head at close range.

2

MILK'S SECRET

Had Harvey Milk not been gay, he probably would have lived an ordinary life. After all, he worked for many years as a math teacher, for an insurance company, and even on Wall Street. Not until the 1960s, when he was in his late thirties, did he realize that he could no longer live a conventional lifestyle. He moved to San Francisco, changed his appearance, and became open about his homosexuality. If he had not embraced radical, confrontational politics, he might still be alive today. But few people would know his name.

Harvey Bernard Milk was born in Woodmere, New York, on Long Island, on May 22, 1930. He entered the world with the odds seemingly against him. The Great Depression was just beginning, and the world would be thrown into war in less than a decade. He was also Jewish, and Jews even in New York faced discrimination and bigotry. As Harvey grew up, he would learn that two-thirds of the Jews in Europe had been murdered by the Nazis and their collaborators.

Fortunately for Harvey's family, they were able to avoid troubled times. Harvey's paternal grandfather, Morris Milch, had emigrated from Lithuania to the United States and, in 1882, opened his own business. Milk's Dry Goods in Woodmere eventually became the largest dry goods store on Long Island.

Morris and his wife had six children, including the hot-tempered William, who served in the Navy during World War I. After the war, William married Minnie Karns,

Young Harvey Milk on a pony

(Courtesy of the Estate of Harvey Milk)

Harvey and Robert Milk at Coney Island on September 1, 1942
(Courtesy of the Estate of Harvey Milk)

a small but determined woman who also served in the Navy during the global conflict. The couple raised two sons: Robert, who was born in 1926, and Harvey. The youngest boy inherited the temperamental nature of his father and the independent spirit of his mother.

With his father working at Milk's Dry Goods, Harvey Milk enjoyed a comfortable childhood. He played cowboys and Indians and various sports. He liked to watch *The Lone Ranger* at the matinées. Harvey attended Hebrew school, and was barmitzvahed when he turned thirteen.

Harvey was gangly with large feet, big ears and a large nose. Yet he was by no means homely. His warm, charming smile was captivating and his energy and sense of humor brightened people's day. Harvey loved to joke around, pull pranks, and make people laugh.

About the only thing unusual about young Harvey was his love of opera. As an adolescent, he often asked his mother for change so that he could go to Saturday afternoon performances at the Metropolitan Opera in Manhattan. He initially just loved the music, but after awhile he began to feel akin to the men standing next to him. He discovered that the Met's standing section was a hangout for homosexuals. More and more, Harvey felt that he was like them.

Concerned about Harvey's getaways to downtown, and the opera, Harvey's mother sat down with him for a serious talk. She told him to stay away from homosexual men, whom, she warned, did unspeakable things with young boys. Harvey was soon full of internal conflicts. Would he develop into one of those deviants whom his mother talked about? How could he live a regular life even though he was different? How could he tell his mother he was gay after she told him not to even go near one of them?

Harvey decided to do what many young homosexuals did—not tell his family and friends. By age fourteen, Harvey was hanging out in New York City's Central Park, where many gay soldiers and other homosexuals gathered. He continued to lead this secret life until 1945, when World War II ended and the family moved to Bayshore, another town on Long Island.

Bayshore was thirty more miles away from Manhattan, making Harvey's trip more difficult. While his father ran Bayshore Furriers, Harvey worked part-time and attended Bayshore High School. At least a couple boys in the school were noticeably gay, but Harvey was not one of them. In fact, Glimpy, as he was called, fit right in. He loved to socialize, contributing to the junior variety show and the junior prom committee. He played linebacker on the junior varsity football team and was a hard-working member of the school basketball team. He even wrestled for a bit, which certainly would have caused a mini-scandal had people known he was gay.

Central Park, New York City
(Courtesy of Jon Arnold Images Ltd / Alamy)

Harvey wasn't part of the popular crowd. Yet classmates remember him as a fun-loving prankster who loved to dance with girls at the local hangout.

"He was funny as heck," said Patrick Vesey, a football teammate of Harvey. "We never dreamt he was gay. . . . We'd go out frequently in a car with a can of beer, driving around, going to parties, and he was right with us—a regular guy."

Harvey's friends were amazed by his brazen actions. Vesey remembered how Harvey once showed up uninvited to a stranger's house party and proceeded to fit right in. In school Harvey was an average student, but one friend felt that there was something special about him.

"I think that Harvey was deeper than we were," said Peggy Meyers Stafford, "more mature in his head in a way. . . . The other guys were always horsing around, everything was fun and games. There was just something about Harvey that led me to believe there was more to him than what he led on, but wasn't about to share with us."

Surely, Harvey's many encounters with older men—those from a subculture much different from the mainstream—gave him a unique perspective on the world. During his high school years, he spent less time in Manhattan and more on Fire Island. Many celebrities and high-society types took a ferry from Bayshore to the island, where they enjoyed the beautiful beaches. It had also become a popular spot for gay men. Harvey liked the company of the older men, even if it was just for conversation.

In 1947, Harvey graduated high school with his secret still intact. The yearbook editors took a shot at his chattiness. The words beneath his photo read: "And they say WOMEN are never at a loss for words!"

On a hot summer day in 1947, Harvey's homosexuality nearly landed him in jail. While hanging out at Central Park without their shirts on, Harvey and other gay men were confronted by police. They were cited for indecent exposure, even though heterosexual men were walking shirtless throughout the park. The arrest was meant to scare the men; the public and politicians didn't want gay men congregating in the park. Harvey was released without serving jail time.

Harvey Milk
"Glimpy"
And they say WOMEN are never at a loss for words!

High school friends remember Milk as extro-verted, scrappy, and a regular guy. *(Courtesy of Bay Shore High School, Bay Shore, New York)*

After high school, Milk was accepted at the New York State College for Teachers in Albany. With so many wartime soldiers enrolling in college, the school didn't have enough housing for everyone. Milk and other male students had to live in barracks, with Milk's bunk next to the bathroom.

Milk continued to conceal his homosexuality. His mother was undoubtedly proud of her son. He majored in math and minored in history, joined a Jewish fraternity, and played intramural football and basketball. He was also a sportswriter for the *State College News* and eventually become the newspaper's sports editor.

Though he joked with the young men and women on campus, Milk didn't have close friends. He touched a lot of people's lives, but only temporarily. He graduated in 1951, leaving Albany without any known friends.

At the time, the United States was involved in the Korean War. Milk believed in the cause—to prevent the Soviet Union from spreading communism throughout Asia. Shortly after graduation, he voluntarily enlisted in the U.S. Navy.

An athletic, smart, and energetic sailor, Milk was considered officer material. Within a year of enlistment, he entered Officers Candidate

Harvey Milk with his mother Minerva and father
William at his college graduation on June 17, 1951.
(Courtesy of the Estate of Harvey Milk)

School in Rhode Island. He rose to the ranks of communications officer, lieutenant junior grade, and chief petty officer aboard the USS *Kittiwake*, an aircraft carrier that patrolled the Pacific. Milk became an excellent deep-sea diver, eventually teaching the skill to other sailors.

In the military at the time, thousands of men were dishonorably discharged because of their sexual orientation. Though Milk hung out with

Harvey Milk in his Navy dress whites, circa 1955
(Courtesy of the San Francisco Public Library)

other gay sailors, he managed to serve a full four years in the Navy. By 1955, however, he was fed up with Navy life and anxious to enter the "real world."

For gay men, the 1950s were a scary time to be entering the workforce. America had never been very accepting of homosexuals, and the Cold War exacerbated conditions. In the wake of World War II, Americans feared that the Soviet Union would spread communism to more countries—perhaps even to the United States. The most paranoid government officials linked communism to Jews, liberals, gays, and other undesirable people who weren't mainstream American.

In 1951, Guy Burgess and Donald MacLean, two homosexual double agents involved in British intelligence, fled to the Soviet Union. For some people, this "proved" that homosexuality was linked to communism. U.S. Senator Joe McCarthy fueled the "Red Scare" when he claimed that the U.S. federal government was riddled with Communists and Communist sympathizers. McCarthy's chief counsel, Roy Cohn, grilled suspected Communists about their sexual orientation. In the early 1950s, dozens of people suspected of being gay were fired in the State Department and throughout the federal government.

In 1953, President Dwight Eisenhower issued Executive Order 10450. The new law stated that federal workers could be dismissed for, among other things, "sexual perversion." Not only were gay government workers fired, but so were those in the private workforce—largely because the government shared its investigative records with private companies.

In the late 1940s, the American Psychiatric Community classified homosexuality as a mental illness. Though no legitimate doctor today believes in that conclusion, that was the thinking in the 1950s. Many gay men tried to live straight lives, only to be persistently "troubled" by their attraction to men. Doctors tried to "cure" homosexuals through counseling, drugs, and even lobotomies—a crude brain operation that often resulted in severe mental disabilities.

During the conservative 1950s, the general public considered homosexuality deviant and sinful. Gay men and women could be arrested for engaging in homosexual acts—even in the privacy of their own homes.

In 1935, the state of Michigan passed the nation's first sexual psychopath law, and by 1967 as many as twenty-six states and the District of Columbia had passed similar laws. There was no clear definition of a sexual psychopath, but psychiatrists, law enforcement officials, and the courts generally applied the label to any person who couldn't control his sexual impulses, or who had a criminal propensity to commit a sex offense. This meant a broad range of people, everyone from so-called "homosexual deviates" to psychotics and peeping toms, could be locked in a mental institution, or in extreme cases, even castrated.

Such cases were rare. Nevertheless, in cities throughout the United States, police routinely raided gay bars and arrested gay men who gathered in parks. Such law enforcement made socializing difficult and dangerous for gay men.

Harvey Milk and other homosexuals were afraid to reveal their secret. In the 1950s, very few gays and lesbians dared to publicly challenge the discriminatory laws. The Mattachine Society and ONE, Inc., both formed in Los Angeles in the early '50s, tried to bring gays together and attempted to speak out against injustices. But these groups were small and nearly powerless in their early years.

After his discharge from the Navy, Milk returned to Long Island and taught math at George W. Hewlett High School. Andrew Marks remembered the young teacher as a "warm, lovable guy . . . a funny, fun-loving, bouncy-type guy." Fellow student Shelly Kamer Roth had a crush on the charismatic teacher. "I was just crazy for him . . . ," Roth said. "He had such a kindness to him. He made you feel special." He was also more handsome than ever. After the Navy, he had undergone plastic surgery to have his famously large nose finely sculpted.

Despite his popularity, Milk lost interest in teaching after the 1956-57 school year. He also was rooming with a young, handsome man named Joe Campbell. If school officials became aware of their relationship, he easily could have been fired.

Wanting to move someplace warm, Milk and Campbell relocated to Dallas in September 1957. Milk, though, found that it was hard for a Jew to find work in Texas. He took a job selling used sewing machines.

Fed up with the job and the city, he and Campbell soon moved back to New York, where Milk landed a job with the Great American Insurance Company, working as an actuarial statistician. Campbell painted furniture. Together they made $330 a week—great money at the time. Sharing an apartment, the couple regularly attended the opera and ballet. Milk told his parents, now in ill health, that Campbell was a friend.

Milk and Campbell were together for nearly seven years, making it the longest relationship Milk would ever have. But Milk was a restless sort, and given to fits of anger. Once, when a man at a restaurant uttered the word "faggot," Milk grabbed him by the collar, shook him hard, and cursed him out. Another time, Milk browbeat a man from Germany (a friend of Campbell's) who had said he was unaware of the Holocaust until after the war. "How could you not have been aware of the carnage?" Milk questioned. "Huh? Were you deaf? Dumb? Blind? Huh?"

Harvey Milk on the Plymouth Savoy in which he and Joe Campbell moved to Texas in 1957
(Courtesy of the Estate of Harvey Milk)

By 1962, Milk had become bored with his job and frustrated with his relationship. He asked Campbell to move out. Milk soon regretted the request, but it was too late. Campbell never came back.

Milk soon found another boyfriend, Craig Rodwell, but their relationship gradually soured. Milk thought that Rodwell was too open about his homosexuality. The young man handed out flyers for the Mattachine Society and challenged police officers who harassed him. Rodwell criticized Milk for not coming out to his parents and for being afraid to hold hands in public. Milk was still not willing to live an openly gay lifestyle, and the couple broke up. Shortly thereafter, Rodwell attempted suicide by overdosing on pills. He survived and Milk visited him in the hospital. Both men would go their separate ways, but each would become famous for the same reason—as activists for gay rights.

In 1963, Milk started life anew. He abruptly quit his insurance job and became a researcher for Bache & Company, a Wall Street investment firm. He also found a new lover, a teenager named Jack McKinley, who eventually moved in with him.

At Bache, Milk concealed his homosexuality. Although he was cocky and always cracking jokes, he excelled at the company. His business insights were fresh and on target and the company rewarded him with healthy raises. But while he succeeded, the loves in his life despaired.

McKinley drank heavily, took drugs, and battled depression. Twice he attempted suicide, including walking into traffic while on a walk with Milk. Then Joe Campbell tried to kill himself. Milk spent days at the hospital waiting for his former lover to recover.

Thinking that McKinley should get away from the vices of New York, Milk accepted a transfer to Bache's office in Dallas. But McKinley soon moved back to New York. Milk found a new young boyfriend, Joe Turner, but he too proved mentally unstable. On more than one occasion, Turner locked himself in the bathroom with a knife and threatened to kill himself.

Once again, Milk was dissatisfied with his life. He transferred back to the New York office in 1968, then resigned after five years at the company.

By the late 1960s, American culture had changed dramatically. The Vietnam War, in which eighteen-year-olds were drafted into the military and sent to Vietnam, alienated young people across the country. Suits and ties, crew-cuts, obeying the rules—all these conservative mores were rejected by many of America's rebellious youth.

In 1968, McKinley was the stage manager for a spectacular Broadway production called *Hair*. This counterculture play reflected the times, with long-haired hippies, flag burning, drug use, a nude scene, and themes of pacifism and environmentalism. Milk, who was friends not only with McKinley but with the play's director, Tom O'Horgan, hung out with the cast and crew.

More and more, Milk's image began to change. He grew his hair longer and longer. Once a political conservative, he adopted more liberal views. His mother had passed away, he rarely saw his father and brother anymore, and he no longer worked on Wall Street. Thus, he no longer had to maintain the "straight" façade.

Self-expression and liberation characterized the cultural revolution of the late 1960s. Women traded their dresses and restrictive bras for more comfortable outfits. Black men and women began to wear African-style clothing. Disgruntled Christians turned to alternative religions—and gays and lesbians became more open about their sexuality.

These changes were most noticeable in San Francisco, the epicenter of the counterculture. When McKinley landed a job as stage director for the San Francisco production of *Hair*, Milk went with him.

It was there, in the City by the Bay, that Milk would find his calling.

Opposite Page: Concert-goers sit on the roof of a Volkswagen bus at the Woodstock Music and Arts Fair at Bethel, New York, in mid-August 1969. The three-day concert attracted hundreds of thousands of people, and became a landmark cultural event of the late '60s.
(Courtesy of AP Images)

3

WINDS OF CHANGE

In May 1848, Sam Brannon ran through the streets of San Francisco yelling, "Gold! Gold! Gold from the American River!" The California gold rush was about to begin, and the city would never be the same.

From 1848 to 1850, San Francisco's population soared from 1,000 to 50,000. Moreover, its population was unlike any in the world. Thousands of gold-seekers, from North America and faraway countries, poured into the city. The great majority of them were male, and these hardened bachelors spent their evenings gambling and drinking in bars and brothels. Over the years, in the city's seedy Barbary Coast, gay restaurants began to emerge.

After the massive earthquake of 1906, the city tried to clean up its image, and Prohibition (1920-33) meant the end of gay bars. Nevertheless, thousands of gay soldiers settled in the city during World War II. The U.S. military did not want homosexuals among its ranks, and tens of thousands of gays were discharged—their papers stamped with an H. Most of the ousted soldiers—those who had served in the Pacific—were given their walking papers in San Francisco. Afraid or unwilling to go home, many stayed in the City by the Bay.

Though there was comfort in numbers, life was often traumatic for the gay men of San Francisco. Gay bars opened after the war, yet laws stated that it was illegal for bars to serve homosexuals, so conflict was inevitable. The city's police force, which was influenced by conservative politicians and the city's powerful Catholic Church leaders,

View of San Francisco harbor, 1851

cracked down on gay bars. Raids, arrests, and intimidation became the norm. When the owner of the Black Cat Café lost his liquor license for serving homosexuals, he took his case to the California Supreme Court. He won, overturning the law.

Yet in the 1950s and '60s, police harassment continued. Many gay bars were closed, and in one famous raid in 1964, more than a hundred people were arrested. The next day, a handful of gay men formed the Society for Individual Rights (SIR). Within three years, SIR membership swelled to 1,200—an impressive number considering the long-standing fear of being outed. San Francisco's gay population was on the verge of being a force in local politics.

In the mid-1960s, a counterculture began to flourish in San Francisco. Repulsed by the Vietnam War and inspired by the African American civil rights movement, thousands of young people embraced the alternative hippie lifestyle. Peace, love, and rock 'n' roll was their credo. Long hair, beards, drugs, Eastern philosophy, and loose-fitting garments adopted from other cultures characterized the hippies as well.

Because of the large gay population and the hippie culture, San Francisco was derided by conservatives as the "kook capital." But for Harvey Milk, who had lived uncomfortably in middle-class America all his life, San Francisco was exciting and liberating.

Milk and Jack McKinley moved to San Francisco in 1969. McKinley soon went back to New York to work on Tom O'Horgan's next blockbuster theatrical production, *Jesus Christ Superstar*, but Milk stayed and took a job at an investment firm. Milk, though, had changed too much to ever again be comfortable in a corporate culture. When told to cut his hair, he refused and was fired.

Despite his fondness for San Francisco, Milk—perpetually restless—moved to Texas and then back to New York. He was no longer the Wall Street hot shot; far from it. In fact, writer John Gruen, in a 1972 *New York Times Magazine* article about O'Horgan, seemed to portray Milk as a pathetic hanger-on:

> A knock at the door. It's Harvey Milk, a longtime friend of O'Horgan's, and a general aide on all of his productions. About O'Horgan's age, Harvey Milk is a sad-eyed man—another aging hippie with long, long hair, wearing faded jeans and pretty beads; he seems to be instinctively attuned to all of O'Horgan's needs. He's come to pick us up. . . . "There is nothing to drink and nothing to eat," O'Horgan tells me. Harvey Milk volunteers to run out for coffee, Cokes and Danish. In a few minutes he reappears with the food.

Despite Gruen's portrayal of Milk, he was seemingly content with his new lifestyle. He was also more than a mere "aide." For O'Horgan's new Broadway play, the controversial *Inner City*, he served as associate producer. His job was to raise money to keep *Inner City* afloat. The play bombed, however, so in 1972 Milk was on the move again. He and his new boyfriend, a young blond Mississippian named Scott Smith, headed to California.

In Milk's Dodge Charger, Milk and Smith spent almost a year bumming around the Golden State. They lived off their unemployment checks and enjoyed the natural beauty of the state, each other's company, their dog (named The Kid), and giant jigsaw puzzles.

When their savings was nearly exhausted, they realized it was time to go back to work. They decided to settle in San Francisco, the city in which Milk was most comfortable. The Castro Street neighborhood was affordable, and filled with considerable gay nightlife. In fact, by the early 1970s, the Castro had become the central gay neighborhood in San Francisco. It was there that Milk and Scott would rent their apartment.

This time, Milk didn't bother with a job interview. After a local pharmacy had ruined his roll of film, he decided to open his own camera store. What did Milk know about cameras?, Smith wondered. Not much, but Milk's father and grandfather had been store owners, and he had a good head for business.

The couple leased a storefront on Castro, moved upstairs, and opened Castro Camera. On March 3, 1973, Milk put a sign in his window: "Yes, We Are Very Open."

Milk's sign implied that more than just the camera store was open. Milk and Smith were announcing that they were "very open" about their homosexuality.

After being in the closet for decades, Milk was now trumpeting to the world that he was gay. To make such an announcement in the Castro neighborhood was largely acceptable, but still a bit dangerous. San Francisco, and Castro in particular, was undergoing volcanic social changes that were either liberating or cataclysmic—depending on one's perspective.

Harvey Milk sharing some intimate moments with Scott Smith at Castro Camera in spring 1976. (Courtesy of Dan Nicoletta)

San Francisco's hippie and gay cultures—each of which were the strongest in the country—were only two parts of the story. Beginning in the 1960s, the city's industries were changing as well. For generations, the San Francisco economy had relied on its busy ports and heavy manufacturing. But during the '60s and '70s, the port traffic declined and many manufacturers moved their plants to the suburbs.

Money-minded city leaders didn't mind, as they envisioned a more lucrative future for San Francisco—one based on white-collar jobs in downtown businesses along with an increase in tourism. Their path would be successful, as the city would become one of the wealthiest in the country, per capita, in the 1980s and '90s. Moreover, tourists would flock by the thousands, year-round, to enjoy San Francisco's many charms: mild weather, ocean views, diverse culture (including a dynamic Chinatown), beautiful architecture, harrowing hills and cable cars, and wonderful dining, lodging, and nightlife.

But as the city forged its new path, others were left out in the cold. The blue-collar minorities—African Americans and Hispanics—who had worked at the city factories couldn't afford to move or commute to the new plants in the suburbs. Although the downtown corporations flourished, their workers tended to commute from the suburbs. The neighborhoods began to die. The Castro was among the city's dying neighborhoods—which is the reason a nearly broke Harvey Milk could afford to move there.

Back in the 1930s, the Castro had flourished as a working-class neighborhood with a large Irish Catholic population. Family life was centered on work, school, and church, all of which were nearby. While minorities tended not to follow factory jobs to the suburbs, the Irish—many of whom had good-paying union jobs—did move to the burbs. Such "white flight" occurred throughout America in the late 1960s and beyond. Well-paid whites left city neighborhoods partly for the lure of the burgeoning suburbs, sometimes for jobs, and often because of their aversion to the growing minority populations in their city neighborhoods.

For each of these reasons, the Irish fled Castro. Thousands of gays and lesbians moved in. Many of the new gay residents had good jobs, but the Castro was still in many ways a deteriorating area—a fact that troubled Harvey Milk, a proponent of strong neighborhoods. Even more troubling was that gays—even after the success of the black civil rights movement and in the city with the largest gay population—continued to face police harassment.

In the late 1960s, a growing segment of the American population recognized that many minorities, not just African Americans, were being denied true equal rights. The women's movement took a significant leap forward with the establishment of the National Organization for Women in 1966. Cesar Chavez and his supporters furthered the rights of Latino and Filipino laborers after organizing a successful strike of grape growers and the California wineries.

In San Francisco, liberal politicians began to champion the rights of the city's gay population. These political leaders not only believed in equal rights for all, but they improved their chances of getting elected, since the city's many homosexuals would cast their votes for them.

Dianne Feinstein was the first notable San Francisco politician to support gay rights and to court the gay vote. A well-to-do woman who had attended both Catholic and Jewish schools, Feinstein ran for a position on the city's Board of Supervisors in 1969. She not only won the election, she garnered more votes than any of the other elected supervisors, thus earning the position of president of the board. In 1971, she courted gays during her run for mayor. She lost to incumbent Joseph Alioto, a Catholic conservative who concentrated on downtown development.

Also in 1971, pro-gay police officer Richard Hongisto shocked the police force when he ran for sheriff—and won. The San Francisco Police Department had been notoriously hard on homosexuals, harassing and arresting thousands throughout the city. They still raided gay bars, and they rounded up gay men who had sex in city parks. Gays, Latinos, and other minorities helped vote Hongiso into office, and he responded by hiring the department's first gay and lesbian officers. Another step forward occurred in 1972, when the Board of Supervisors passed a law that banned discrimination against gays by city contractors.

Gay men and women themselves were also making headway in San Francisco politics. In 1971, lesbian couple Del Martin and Phyllis Lyon formed the Alice B. Toklas Memorial Democratic Club (known as Alice). Gay activist Jim Foster, who years earlier had been discharged from the Army because he was gay, became the club's president and a prominent spokesperson.

When U.S. Senator George McGovern, a liberal, pro-gay Democrat from South Dakota, ran for president in 1972, Alice workers campaigned hard for him in California. McGovern returned the favor by allowing Foster to speak at the Democratic National Convention—on national television. It was an extraordinary moment for the fledgling gay rights movement. No openly gay person had ever been granted such a platform.

In his speech, Foster noted the injustices that gay Americans still endured. He discussed the police crackdowns on gay bars, the purges of gays in the military, and the fact that the U.S. Civil Service Commission still spent $12 million a year to investigate suspected gay federal employees. Foster didn't expect laws to change overnight, but he urged people to be aware of the injustices and respect the rights of gays and lesbians.

"We do not come to you pleading your understanding or begging your tolerance," Foster declared. "We come to you affirming our pride in our lifestyle, affirming the validity to seek and to maintain meaningful emotional relationships, and affirming our right to participate in the life of this country on an equal basis with every citizen."

The gays of San Francisco celebrated Foster's speech, yet they knew that so much more needed to be done. They were still ostracized, even in America's "gay capital," and local authorities still classified homosexuality as a crime. They were supposed to feel ashamed of themselves. Many were too afraid to come out, suffering instead with intense loneliness and other painful emotions.

Even in San Francisco, few politicians thought that gays were ready to run for public office. The Alice organization preferred instead to work within the Democratic Party, urging straight politicians to support the gay agenda.

For Milk, this cautious path wasn't enough. Now in his forties, he was tired of waiting for the straight society to grant gays their constitutional rights. He had seen too many of his friends ridiculed, arrested, and sink into suicidal depression.

In 1973, after spending so many years as a restless drifter, Milk decided it was time to enter politics. He would do so as an openly gay man, and he would urge others to be proud of who they were. He would run for a seat on San Francisco's Board of Supervisors, where he would push for gay rights and also address the needs of the city's neglected neighborhoods.

"Harvey spent most of his life looking for a stage," said his friend Tom O'Horgan. "On Castro Street, he finally found it."

Harvey Milk at the Gay Pride Celebration, June 30, 1974, at the
San Fransisco Civic Center. He was selling raffle tickets.
(Courtesy of Don Eckert)

4 THE MAYOR OF CASTRO STREET

Harvey Milk would eventually become a politician with high ideals. Yet it wasn't "liberty" and "democracy" that sparked his run for city supervisor. It was a state tax, a broken slide projector, and Watergate.

Shortly after Milk opened Castro Camera in 1973, a state official walked into his store to announce that he couldn't operate unless he paid a $100 fee to the state. Milk, a longtime believer in free enterprise, felt that the government was suppressing the small businessman. "You mean I have to be wealthy to operate a business in the state of California?" Milk asked. The official wouldn't budge, and their conversation escalated into a shouting match. For weeks, Milk argued with state bureaucrats, fuming about the fee.

No longer feeling constrained by society, Milk was more vocal than ever. When a high school teacher came into the store asking to borrow a slide projector because the school didn't have one, Milk went ballistic. How could the city spend millions of dollars catering to the needs of downtown corporations, he declared, but couldn't afford the most basic equipment for its schools?

The Watergate hearings convinced Milk that something was seriously wrong in American politics. In 1972, five men had been arrested for breaking into the Democratic National Committee headquarters at the Watergate Office complex in Washington, D.C. Investigators gradually discovered that the break-in was

The Castro Theater is an icon in San Francisco's Castro District

(Courtesy of Eli Katsumata / Alamy))

Named in the Watergate affair were from left to right: G. Gordon Liddy, White House Counsel John W. Dean III, former Attorney General John N. Mitchell, and former Deputy Campaign Manager for Nixon's reelection Jeb Stuart Magruder. (Courtesy of AP Images)

part of a wider scheme of illegal activity by President Richard Nixon and his 1972 reelection campaign. During hearings held by the U. S. Senate, Attorney General John Mitchell repeatedly dodged questions from the senators about his involvement in Watergate. Milk, watching the daily hearings in his shop, screamed at the television.

Upset, Milk was now ready to run for public office. His goal was a seat on San Francisco's Board of Supervisors, the eleven-member legislative branch of San Francisco's government. Each member represented a district, and Milk would run for the seat that included the Castro neighborhood.

Milk didn't enter the race until August 1973, just three months before the election. He belonged to no organization, and he had no constituents he had to please. He was merely an average citizen running for office. Milk relished this role. In fact, Milk began his campaign by walking to the local plaza with a few supporters, standing on a crate, and announcing his candidacy.

Afterward, Milk told a reporter that it was time for him to "get involved and do something about the things that are wrong in this society. I've got to fight not just for me but for my lover and his next lover eventually. It's got to be better for them than it was for me."

Milk was impressive in interviews, and the media considered him a terrific story subject. After all, here was a Jewish hippie, with a beard and a ponytail—with loads of charisma and a gift of gab—who was fighting for the little guy. On top of that, this candidate was gay, which was a rarity even in San Francisco.

Milk also had an attention-grabbing platform. Naturally, he favored legislation that would improve gay rights, specifically an end to government interference in private sexual matters. But his platform ran the gamut. He believed that the city should invest its revenue in high-yield funds—a reflection of his days on Wall Street. On the other end of the spectrum, he called for the legalization of marijuana—a reflection of his hippie lifestyle. He also believed that city workers should take buses to work each day.

Milk was a populist politician, meaning someone who puts the needs of the common people ahead of the privileged elite. As such, he strongly supported a ballot proposition that called for district elections for the Board of Supervisors. At the time, every voter in San Francisco could vote for all the supervisor candidates. In other words, if you lived in District 1, you could vote for the candidate in your district and for those in the ten other districts.

Critics argued that this system was corrupt. They claimed that wealthy businessmen—those who favored downtown corporate development—would financially support those board candidates who catered to their interests. Those candidates would then emerge as the front-runners because they would have the most money to spend on their campaigns. Thus, the board would be dominated by those who cared most about the big businesses, and not about the neighborhood residents.

Despite Milk's pro-gay agenda, and the fact that he was one of the few gays willing to run for office, the Alice B. Toklas Memorial Democratic Club did not support him. In fact, Alice President Jim Foster resented Milk because he considered him to be an outsider who had no right to run for such a prestigious office. Foster and his colleagues had been toiling in city politics for years. Why should Milk be the one to become San Francisco's first openly gay city supervisor?

Foster told Milk that he should be patient. He also told Milk that the city wasn't yet ready for a gay supervisor. Gay progress in San Francisco, Foster believed, had to be gradual. Otherwise, there could be a backlash. The city was still run by a powerful conservative administration headed by Mayor Joseph Alioto.

Milk refused to quit. He believed a gay candidate who had access to the media on a daily basis could educate the public about the need for all citizens to be treated equally. Moreover, Milk thought, gay candidates would serve as role models to younger homosexuals, improving their self-esteem, inspiring them to "come out," and emboldening them to become active in politics.

Foster and Milk were clearly not in agreement. Milk would have to win his election on his own, without the support of Alice. Though the odds were stacked against him, Milk forged ahead. He was supported by gays on the fringe of society, such as drag queens. Some gay bar owners, who were angry that Alice had done little to prevent police harassment, supported him as well.

Despite few campaign donations, Milk and Scott Smith did their best to promote Milk. They created and distributed press releases that announced endorsements. Performing Artists for Milk, chaired by Smith, was in reality a flimsy endorsement, but at least it was something. Milk kept plugging away.

"You could see the assertive look on his face as he approached several of us at the bar," recalled Castro resident Ron Williams. "He was handing out flyers and buttons for some political thing. . . . I remember the hair, ponytail, strong eyes and friendly handshake. . . . His political strategy was to get gay people to register to vote and get them involved in the political process. . . . [P]eople started to pay attention and Harvey's political momentum began to build."

Milk knew that gays in the Castro would vote for him, and that he was faring well in his interviews. For a first-time candidate with a shoestring budget, he had reason to be proud.

Opposite Page: Harvey Milk at the opening of the 1975 campaign for supervisor. (Courtesy of San Francisco Public Library)

On election night, Milk and a few friends watched the results on television in a Chinese restaurant. Among the thirty-two candidates for the Board of Supervisors, he received nearly 17,000 votes and finished in tenth place—not high enough to win the seats that were available.

Despite the lost, Milk had reason to be optimistic. He had done extremely well among hippies and the students of San Francisco State University. More importantly, he was the leading vote-getter in the Castro area. Milk felt that if elections could one day be switched from citywide to district—and there already was a great deal of support for such a scenario—he would win his coveted supervisor position.

In his concession speech, Milk vowed to run again. He also declared that gays should strive to win political office on their own. They should no longer simply support straight liberal Democrats, hoping for "a crumb thrown to keep us happy . . . when in reality we should be getting our freedom."

"I have tasted freedom," he said. "I will not give up that which I have tasted. I have a lot more to drink."

Shortly after the election, Milk cut his long hair. He also vowed to abstain from marijuana and avoid San Francisco's bathhouses, where gay men met for sexual trysts. He did so because mainstream voters disdained all three of these factors.

After the 1973 elections, Milk discovered that he didn't have to hold public office to make a difference. His camera shop became the political epicenter of Castro's growing gay community. Those with a cause, be it related to gay rights or the environment, taped flyers to the store's front window and left literature on the counter. Milk urged his customers to register to vote and cajoled his friends into becoming registrars. Those in the neighborhood knew that Milk was the guy to see if you had a question about filing a grievance with the police or city hall.

While his partner, Scott Smith, tended the store, Milk canvassed the neighborhood, introducing himself to fellow businessmen, be it straight or gay. As such, he opened much-needed dialogue between the old-time Catholics and the "queers" whom they felt were "taking over" the neighborhood. For Milk, making new friends was great for his business and his political ambitions. He also had a genuine interest in strengthening the community—and, of course, he loved to talk.

One person in the neighborhood, Tory Hartmann, found out just how outgoing and kind Milk could be. Milk barely knew Hartmann, but when he heard that she recently had suffered a miscarriage, he came to help.

"Lo and behold, there was a knock at the door . . . ," Hartmann said. "And he was standing on my doorstep with a dozen roses, and then he said, 'Well, can I get you anything? Do you have enough food in the house? Do you have milk? Do you have food? I'll do your grocery shopping.' And I knew him by name, but I didn't know him well enough to do my grocery shopping. But that's the kind of concern he [had]."

In the months after the 1973 elections, Milk became known as the "Mayor of Castro Street." It was an unofficial title, of course, but Milk cherished it and would tout himself as such in future interviews.

Some began to view Milk as more of a local miracle worker than a mayor. Although he didn't exactly turn water into wine, he did make beer disappear.

One day, Teamsters representative Allan Baird stopped by the camera store to ask a big favor from Milk. The local beer-truck drivers were on strike, he said, because the six major beer distributors wouldn't adhere to their union's demands. Baird had convinced Arab and Chinese grocers to stop buying beer from those six distributors, and now he was asking Milk to exert his influence on the gay community.

Milk was inclined to support the local union men, and he also saw an opportunity. He said he would help organize the strike if the Teamsters would start hiring gay truck drivers. "You've got to promise me one thing," he told Baird. "You've got to help bring gays into the Teamsters Union. We buy a lot of beer that the union delivers. It's only fair that we get a share of the jobs."

Baird agreed, and the two men went out to fulfill their promises. Milk influenced gay bar owners to stop buying beer from the Big Six, and he drummed up press coverage of the boycott.

With the Arab, Chinese, and now gay communities aiding the boycott, the beer distributors were suffering. Five of the six capitulated to the union demands—a great victory for the Teamsters. Baird was not only grateful for Milk's help, and impressed by Milk's effective leadership, but he was able to convince the Teamsters to hire gay drivers. Milk and Baird would remain friends, and the Teamsters would endorse Milk in a future campaign.

While Milk sometimes extended his hand to the straight community, he often warred against them as well—especially if they showed hostility to homosexuals. Such a situation developed when two gay men tried to open an antique store in the Castro. The Eureka Valley Merchants Association (EVMA), an organization of conservative business owners, urged police to deny the men a license to operate the store. Although the men prevailed in the battle of wills, relations soured between the EVMA and the local gay merchants.

Milk responded by organizing the Castro Village Association (CVA) and became its elected president. Milk urged local gays to buy from gay merchants. To further the cause, he prodded CVA members to launch a Castro Street Fair. Staged in August 1974, it was a rousing success, with thousands of visitors and booming business. Milk further strengthened the CVA by getting the neighborhood banks, Hibernia Bank and Bank of America, to join the association. Considering that the Hibernia was Irish-owned and that Bank of America was the largest bank in the country, this was a major coup.

Milk frequently compared the gay rights movement to the civil rights movement, and in some ways the Castro in 1974 was like Montgomery, Alabama, in 1956. In response to black citizens' assertiveness that year (their boycott of the city buses and of downtown businesses), the Montgomery police amped up their harassment of African Americans. The same thing happened in the Castro in 1974. As more gays "took over" the neighborhood, the police force went on the attack.

Police pulled up to gays on the sidewalk and asked if they were headed to a gay bar. If they indicated that they were, the police arrested them. On some evenings, police rounded up a group of gay men, took them to a park, handcuffed them, and beat them with their nightsticks.

The most alarming raid of all in 1974 occurred in the wee hours of Labor Day. Police stormed Castro Street, grabbing and beating dozens of gay men. They hurled fourteen men into paddy wagons, charging them with obstructing a sidewalk. San Francisco's gay leadership responded with legal action. Attorney Rick Stokes, a local gay rights activist, filed a million-dollar lawsuit against the police department.

Milk, of course, was fuming mad. He launched a defense fund for the victims and lashed out against the police in the media. At a community relations meeting about the incident, he called the police "pigs"—a pejorative term for officers at the time. Thanks partly to Milk's efforts, police harassment died down considerably after the Labor Day incident.

In March 1975, Milk announced that he would once again run for a seat on San Francisco's Board of Supervisors. Six current supervisors were up for reelection, meaning all six seats were up for grabs. Milk didn't have to put gay rights as a showcase item on his agenda; as the only gay candidate, he would dominate the gay vote. Instead, he promised to switch the focus in San Francisco from downtown business interests to neighborhoods and the common folk.

Milk complained that the city was under-assessing hotels and corporate buildings, meaning the owners of those structures were paying less in taxes than they should. That meant that the rest of the city's taxpayers had to pay more. He also believed that the many suburbanites who worked downtown should pay taxes to the city. After all, they virtually lived in the city for eight hours a day. Why should they get a free pass?

Taxing commuters may seem like an unorthodox request, but 1975 was a highly unconventional year in San Francisco politics. Mayor Alioto's second and last term was about to expire, and liberal candidates were poised to take over city hall. Except for white conservatives, seemingly every group in the city was hungry for change.

The billion-dollar construction of the Bay Area Rapid Transit system (BART) had laid waste to a Latino neighborhood. Considering that BART was created to carry suburban workers to their downtown jobs, many Latinos were upset. Chinatown had also been neglected, and many African Americans had lost their jobs due to the closing of neighborhood plants.

The ranks of liberals grew not just in San Francisco but throughout the country. Americans were disgusted with how Washington had handled the Vietnam War, and the Watergate scandal resulted in the 1974 resignation of Republican president Richard Nixon. By 1975, at least in San Francisco, even unions were willing to support a gay candidate.

Through his friend Allan Baird, Milk earned the endorsement of the local Beer Truck Drivers union. More significantly, the Teamsters and the Building and Construction Trades Council endorsed him too. These union leaders were impressed with Milk when they met him, and Milk fully supported the unions' agendas.

The stereotype of union members—closed-minded and homophobic—was being shattered in San Francisco. Union leaders were savvy to the fact that the attitudes of the citizenry were changing, and that the city's gay population was increasing dramatically. Milk, they believed, was on his way to becoming a powerful figure. Even the San Francisco fire fighters supported Milk. Excluding the police, Milk had all the "tough guys" on his side. Many even stopped at his camera store to work for his campaign.

The city was changing so much that a liberal candidate, George Moscone, emerged as the front-runner in the mayoral race. Moscone, who was serving as the majority leader of the California Senate, wanted to govern his native city—it was his childhood dream.

For the liberals and minorities of San Francisco, Moscone was the ideal candidate. He vowed to open city hall to everyone: women, African Americans, Asians, Latinos, and gays. In the California Senate in 1975, he had pushed through a bill that repealed the state's "crimes against nature" law, which among other things, outlawed homosexual sex. This law, which was on the books in many states, allowed police to arrest gays whenever and wherever they participated in sexual activity. Moscone's action was a major breakthrough for gay

Opposite Page: The Bay City Reds juggling troupe at the Castro Street Fair, San Francisco, 1975. Performers are, from left: Dan Mankin, Billy Kessler, Diana, Don Forrest, Merle Goldstone. *(Courtesy of BillyKwiki)*

rights across the country, as other states would soon follow California's lead and repeal the notorious law.

In San Francisco, the times were ripe for a gay city supervisor, and Milk had the right message, the right personality, and strong endorsements. What he didn't have was the money for a large citywide campaign. Milk needed to find a low-cost, creative way to get his name out there. He came up with the "human billboard."

Handsome, young gay men, carrying "Harvey Milk for Supervisor" signs, volunteered to line a street together to promote the candidate. The novel concept attracted the attention of passersby and became a topic of conversation. As Milk planned, newspaper photographers stopped to take pictures, which made the local papers.

As 1975 progressed, Milk found himself in the center of extraordinary and bizarre events. For one thing, the Castro was in the midst of a gay renaissance. After learning that the area was a burgeoning gay center, thousands of homosexuals from all over the country poured into the district in the early and mid-1970s. Many of them renovated their homes, including the large, ornate Victorian houses that characterized the area. The Castro neighborhood became such a hot spot that houses doubled and tripled in value from the early to mid-1970s.

Longtime straight residents sold their houses for big bucks and moved out of the neighborhood, making Castro's gay population even more pronounced. The CVA, with Milk as president, continued to grow, and the 1975 Castro Street Fair attracted more than 20,000 visitors.

Through it all, the gay culture changed dramatically. Men eschewed effeminate traits and went all-out macho. The fashionable wore blue jeans, boots, cowboy hats, construction hats, and army fatigues. The outfits of the gay music group Village People were an exaggerated reflection of this new culture. In fact, two of the group's biggest hits were "San Francisco" and "Macho Man."

Yet not every gay man in San Francisco was so expressive. Oliver "Bill" Sipple, age thirty-three, was a former Marine who kept his homosexuality quiet. He had never told his Baptist mother that he was gay.

In 1975, Sipple worked as a volunteer for Milk's campaign. That itself was ironic, since Sipple was once the romantic partner of Joe Campbell, Milk's lover back in the early 1960s. On September 22, 1975, Sipple stood outside San Francisco's St. Francis Hotel when President Gerald Ford walked out the door. In a frantic moment, Sipple noticed that the

Oliver Sipple, left, lunges for Sara Jane Moore, arrow, after a shot was fired in the direction of President Ford as he left the Hotel St. Francis, in San Francisco, on September 23, 1975. (Courtesy of AP Photo/San Francisco Examiner/Gordon Stone)

woman next to him, cloaked in a raincoat, was pulling out a gun to shoot the president. The woman, Sara Jane Moore, fired a shot and missed. As she aimed for another shot, Sipple grabbed the gun and tackled her.

Sipple might have enjoyed the fame had Milk not become involved. Milk leaked to a reporter that Sipple was gay. When Milk's friend told him he shouldn't be outing Sipple—that it was an invasion of privacy— Milk responded: "It's too good an opportunity. For once we can show that gays do heroic things."

Milk's leak became a national story. It may have helped the gay community, but it had a horribly detrimental effect on Sipple. President Ford refrained from honoring him, and his own mother was so mortified by the "scandal" that she cut off contact with her son for years. Sipple was already, in his words, "screwed up mentally" because of the trauma he had suffered during the Vietnam War.

Sipple sued multiple newspapers and publishers—those who reported that he was gay—for invasion of privacy, but after years in the courts his case was dismissed. He became a heavy drinker, suicidal, and morbidly obese. In 1989, he died while struggling for breath.

Harvey Milk's life had become an unending drama, and election day 1975 was no exception. Milk's friends and supporters joined him at a restaurant to watch the voting results. But on this day, Milk finished just short. All six incumbent supervisors who were running for reelection prevailed. Milk finished a highly respectable seventh in the voting. He faired poorly in the conservative districts, but in the Castro area he again finished No. 1 among all candidates.

As Milk was delivering his concession speech, George Moscone arrived unexpectedly at the restaurant. People rose and cheered the visitor, who had just defeated candidates John Barbagelata (a conservative who opposed the Gay Freedom Day Parade) and Dianne Feinstein (a moderate liberal). Moscone came to show his support for Milk—and the gay community.

Moscone had political as well ideological reasons to support Milk. In San Francisco, the top two finishers in the mayoral election had to face each other in a run-off election in December. By supporting Milk—now the most popular gay man in San Francisco—Moscone could dominate the gay vote in the run-off against Barbagelata. In that second election, Moscone ended up needing every vote he could get, as he won by just 4,400 votes.

In his victory speech, Moscone promised Milk a role in his administration. In fact, all of the minorities who had been excluded from city hall would be welcomed by the new mayor. "He opened the city government up to new people, and different people," said Deputy Mayor Rudy Nothenberg. "There was a pent-up demand for participation by those excluded. George opened the doors."

Moscone pleased minorities by appointing former Oakland police chief Charles Gain as San Francisco's chief of police. Gain was one of the most liberal police chiefs in the country. In San Francisco, he wanted to change the force's image and to hire officers dedicated to serving the entire community. Gain forbade drinking on the job, changed the colors of the patrol cars from black to powder blue, and said he was open to having gays serve on the police force.

None of these changes sat well with many of the officers, who in general hated their new police chief. Before, officers had the green light to beat up gays at random. Now, their chief seemed to display more concern for gays than his own officers.

San Francisco's new liberal leadership hoped that the old-school conservatism would melt away, and that the city would embrace diversity forevermore. Instead, the old power structure quietly seethed, creating a highly charged and potentially dangerous situation.

Political Pioneers

Harvey Milk is often cited as the first openly gay person elected to public office in the United States, but that distinction goes to Kathy Kozachenko. In January 1974, at the age of twenty-two, Kozachenko campaigned for and won a seat on the Ann Arbor (Michigan) city council. Kozachenko filled the seat of Nancy Wechsler, who had come out as a lesbian while serving on the council. Later the same year, Elaine Noble of Boston gained national attention when she was elected to the Massachusetts House of Representatives. Noble endured death threats, shootings through her windows, vandalism of her car, and the breaking of windows at her campaign headquarters. "It was a very ugly campaign," she recalled. Despite the harassment, Noble successfully ran for a second term in 1976, winning with almost 90 percent of the vote. And, Noble's state-level win opened the door for other gay and lesbian politicians. In 1980, Gene Ulrich became America's first openly gay mayor, of a small town in Missouri. Then in 1984, Gerry Studds, a Massachusetts Democrat, was elected to the U.S. House of Representatives. The late Allan Spear holds the record as the longest-serving openly elected politician in America. Spear served almost thirty years in the Minnesota Senate, from 1972 to 2000.

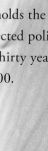

Elaine Noble, May 1975 *(Courtesy of AP Photo)*

MILK VS.
THE MACHINE

Early in 1976, as America celebrated its bicentennial, San Fransisco mayor George Moscone opened a new chapter in the city's history. He appointed a remarkably diverse group of men and women to the Board of Permit Appeals, a commission that had the final say on any permit issued by the city. Included were a Filipino, an African American woman, and a homosexual man— Harvey Milk.

Permit appeals were not exactly what Milk had in mind when he entered politics. He soon began to eye a more powerful position—a seat in the California State Assembly. The Assembly was the state's equivalent of the U.S. House of Representatives, the lower house of the California state legislature.

Friends told Milk to stick with his Permit Appeals position and run again for city supervisor in 1977. With his growing popularity, an expanding gay population, and Moscone's support, Milk likely would win next time. But Milk was too restless. He had always felt that he would die young, and now, at age forty-five, he did not have the patience to wait two more years.

After the 1975 elections, Assemblyman John Foran of California's Sixteenth Assembly District left his post to take over Moscone's vacated state Senate seat. Milk wanted the newly available Assembly seat, which represented the Castro and the other eastern neighborhoods of San Francisco. This was his turf, he felt; there was no question he would win the upcoming election. Or so he thought.

George Moscone
(Courtesy of AP Images)

What Milk didn't know was that Moscone and other California power brokers already had a candidate in mind to assume Foran's Assembly seat. Art Agnos was the chief of staff for Speaker of the Assembly Leo McCarthy and had the support of most of the influential politicians. Milk could run, but Moscone, the powerful McCarthy, and other heavyweights would back Agnos. Moreover, Moscone had a rule in which the city's elected and appointed officials—such as Milk—were not allowed to run for another political office.

Milk felt he was being shut out of the position, by back-room politics. The Assembly seat was an elected position and the mayor and other politicians were trying to sabotage the democratic process. Despite serving on the Board of Permit Appeals for barely a month, and in spite of Moscone's warning that he would be fired if he ran for assemblyman, Milk announced publicly that he would indeed run for the vacated Assembly seat.

In doing so, Milk risked political suicide by antagonizing the leader of his city and the powerful speaker of the Assembly. Moreover, he referred to the powers-that-be as "the machine"—a term with negative connotations. In machine politics, those in charge collude with fellow politicians to maintain their power; outsiders have little chance of being elected.

"I think a representative should earn his or her seat," Milk said during the speech in which he announced he was running. "I don't think the seat should be awarded on the basis of service to the machine. Machines operate on oil and grease; they're dirty, dehumanizing, and too often unrepresentative to any needs but those of the operator."

Almost immediately after Milk's announcement, Moscone removed Milk from the Board of Permit Appeals. The press gave the story a great deal of attention. Milk was now the gay maverick, the little guy taking on the Establishment. He embraced the role, adopting the slogan "Harvey Milk vs. The Machine."

Milk immersed himself into campaigning. He strolled throughout the Sixteenth District, shaking as many hands as he could find. He even resurrected the human billboards, only this time his sign-toting

Giant Harvey Milk for Assembly campaign button at his camera
store in 1976 San Francisco. Milk's reflection is seen in the window.
(Courtesy of Robert Clay/Alamy)

volunteers lined the busy Market Street. As commuters arrived at their
downtown offices, they undoubtedly blurted, "Did you see those guys
with the 'Milk for Assembly' signs?'" Milk knew how to create a buzz.

The Harvey Milk saga grew increasingly bizarre when he encoun-
tered the Peoples Temple. Led by Reverend Jim Jones, the Peoples
Temple was ostensibly a religious organization but in reality a cult.
Jones lured mostly poor people, including many African Americans, to
his "church." They lived in Temple-run communes and participated in
practices such as paddling children and other humiliation rituals—all
in front of church members. No members were allowed to talk about
these practices outside the church.

Milk knew this group was strange, but he spoke at the Peoples Temple, and some of its members made phone calls on behalf of his campaign. Milk told his volunteers: "Make sure you're always nice to the Peoples Temple. If they ask you to do something, do it, and then send them a note thanking them for asking you to do it. They're weird and they're dangerous, and you never want to be on their bad side." For Milk, the bad vibes from the Peoples Temple were a portent of a future tragedy—one that would play out just days before his own assassination.

Milk campaigned as hard as possible for the state Assembly seat. But despite his efforts, he was crushed by the machine in the November 1976 elections. Out of 33,000 ballots cast, Art Agnos won by a convincing 3,600.

Though Milk was defeated, he had reasons to forge ahead. New causes and new possibilities were on the horizon, and he was about to embark on the most fruitful period of his life.

In the same election, San Francisco voters decided to end citywide ballots for Board of Supervisor candidates. In future elections, citizens in one district would vote solely for candidates in their district. Thus, people would have a stronger say in shaping the future of their neighborhoods. This was a huge break for Milk. With the next supervisor election just a year away, Milk would be the overwhelming favorite to win in District 5—the Castro district.

In 1977, Milk disassociated himself even further from the Alice B. Toklas Democratic Club. Milk and other gay activists formed the more aggressive San Francisco Gay Democratic Club. They issued the following statement:

> No decisions which affect our lives should be made without the gay voice being heard. We want our fair share of city services. We want openly gay people appointed and elected to city offices—people who reflect the diversity of our community. We want the schools of San Francisco to provide full exposure to and positive appreciation of gay lifestyles. We are asking no more than we deserve: We will not settle for less.

As Milk worked for progress in San Francisco, he was alarmed by news reports out of Florida. An organized group of Christian activists was trying to repeal gay-rights legislation in Dade County. Gay activists in Miami had convinced legislators in January 1977 to pass an ordinance that banned discrimination—in housing, employment, and public services—based on sexual orientation. Now an organization called Save Our Children was trying to overturn it.

Singer Anita Bryant, who most Americans knew as the TV pitch woman for Florida orange juice, led the campaign. She believed that homosexuality was sinful, and that gays were trying to promote lewd behavior. "What these people really want, hidden behind obscure legal phrases, is the legal right to propose to our children that there is an acceptable alternate way of life," she said. "I will lead such a crusade to stop it as this country has not seen before."

Bryant kept her word. With contributions from the Florida Citrus Commission, the Save Our Children campaign garnered the 10,000 signatures needed for a referendum vote (actually getting more than 60,000 signatures). On June 7, 1977, Dade County residents would go to the polls and decide if they wanted to repeal the gay-rights legislation.

What followed was a well-funded and often ugly anti-gay campaign. A TV ad contrasted the Orange Bowl Parade (which Bryant had hosted many times) with risqué footage from the San Francisco Gay Freedom Day Parade. The ad claimed that Miami was in danger of turning into a hotbed of sexuality, like San Francisco. Moreover, Save Our Children ran ads portraying homosexual men as child molesters. Studies show that homosexuals had no higher incidences of child molestation than did heterosexuals.

Nevertheless, in her speeches leading up to the referendum, Bryant portrayed gay men as pedophiles. "As a mother, I know that homosexuals cannot biologically reproduce children; therefore, they must recruit our children . . . ," she said. "If gays are granted rights, next we'll have to give rights to prostitutes and to people who sleep with St. Bernards and to nail biters."

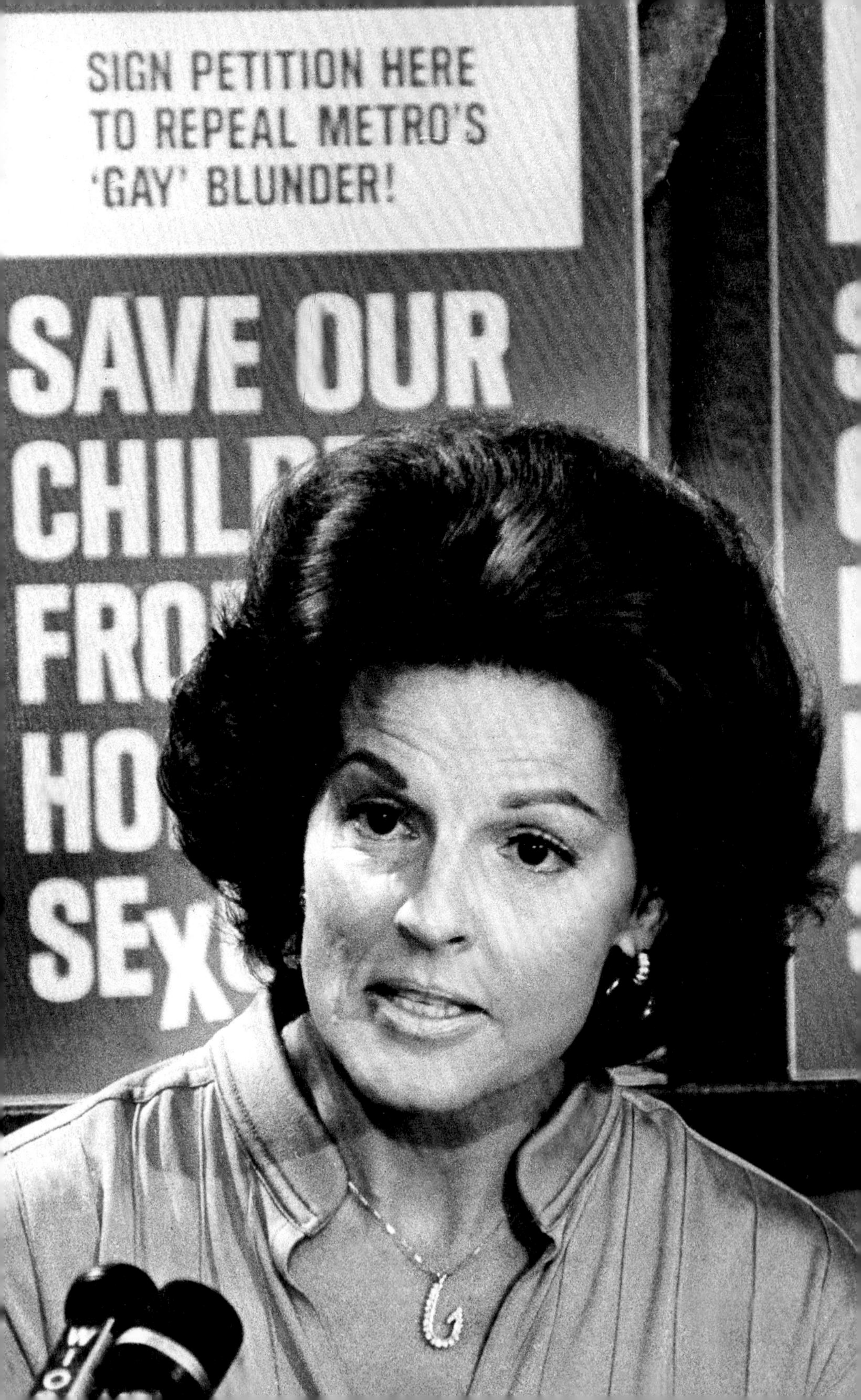
SIGN PETITION HERE
TO REPEAL METRO'S
'GAY' BLUNDER!

Gays fought back by organizing a nationwide boycott on orange juice. For perhaps the first time in American history, discussions of homosexuality saturated the mainstream media. Though fuzzy about the details, elementary school students across the country knew that Anita Bryant didn't like gay people.

The boycott may have hurt juice sales but it did little to counter the salacious propaganda that Save Our Children was peddling. In a huge turnout for the referendum on June 7, Dade County citizens voted by a more than two to one margin to repeal the gay-rights legislation. Elated by the victory, Bryant vowed to repeal similar laws throughout the country.

"All America and all the world will hear what the people have said," Bryant declared, "and with God's continued help, we will prevail in our fight to repeal similar laws throughout the nation which attempt to legitimize a lifestyle that is both perverse and dangerous."

The results of the vote sparked outrage among gay communities. In Greenwich Village in New York City, hundreds of gays and lesbians took to the streets, carrying candles and signs that supported gay rights.

But the biggest demonstration of all took place in San Francisco's Castro district. More than 3,000 Castro residents assembled outdoors, urging gays to come out and join them. Milk took charge, leading the men and women on a five-mile march through the city, letting San Francisco know that homosexuals would not cower in defeat. "This is the power of the gay community," Milk declared to the energized crowd. "Anita's going to create a national gay force!"

Indeed, gays and their supporters rallied to the cause. The day after the Miami vote, gay-rights marches took place in Los Angeles, Houston, Boston, New Orleans, and Indianapolis.

In the days and weeks that followed, Anita Bryant continued to travel and speak out against homosexuality. But wherever she appeared, angry

Opposite Page: Singer and anti-gay activist Anita Bryant crusades to nullify a Miami gay rights ordinance, February 15, 1977. Bryant calls the group Save Our Children and vows it will represent the rights of the majority of citizens. *(Courtesy of AP Images)*

demonstrators greeted her. One activist shoved a strawberry rhubarb pie in her face, bringing her to tears. Those in charge of the Orange Bowl Parade ended her ten-year run as host, and her record company refused to release her upcoming album, *There's Nothing Like the Love Between a Man and a Woman.*

Yet the Save Our Children campaign in Florida sparked similar crusades in other American cities in 1977 and '78. Gay-rights ordinances went up for a repeal vote in Eugene, Oregon; Wichita, Kansas; St. Paul, Minnesota; and Seattle, Washington. In all but Seattle, the laws were overturned.

American gays couldn't believe what was happening. Many compared their oppression to the early years of the Nazi regime, when Hitler gradually stripped away the rights of Jews, gays, and other "outcasts." Some homosexuals committed suicide during these crusades, with their loved ones claiming that the hateful rhetoric led directly to their deaths.

Though the referendums occurred in other states, the shockwaves affected the gays of San Francisco. On June 21, 1977, two weeks after the Dade County election, four men ambushed a gay couple in San Francisco as the two men exited their car. One of the gay men ran for cover, and the attackers focused their hate on the other man—Robert Hillsborough, age thirty-one, who had once registered to vote in Milk's camera store. One of the attackers, a Latino youth, stabbed Hillsborough fifteen times in the chest and face while his friends chanted "faggot, faggot, faggot."

The hate crime sent shudders throughout San Francisco, home to more than 100,000 homosexuals. Mayor Moscone blamed Bryant and John Briggs—an anti-gay California politician—for fanning the flames of hatred. Moscone ordered the flags in the city to be flown at half-mast—an unusual gesture for a street crime.

On June 25, the police announced that they had arrested four men, including the person who allegedly had stabbed Hillsborough to death. He was John Cordova, a nineteen-year-old man from the suburbs. City officials were relieved that the culprits had been apprehended because the Gay Freedom Day Parade was scheduled for June 26. The arrests brought at least some closure to the ordeal.

Due to all the attention surrounding gay rights in 1977, gays and lesbians flocked in huge numbers to the parade. Close to 250,000 people attended, making it as big as the 1963 March on Washington. In their dress and body language, participants let TV audiences know that they were gay and proud of it. Some carried signs asserting their rights and condemning their enemies.

Crowds hailed Harvey Milk, who used the occasion to announce his candidacy for city supervisor in the November 1977 election. He asserted that his victory would be a victory for all gay Americans. "[I]t's not my election I want; it's yours," Milk said to a massive audience. "It will mean that a green light is lit that says to all who feel lost and disenfranchised that you can now go forward. It means hope, and we, no, you and you and you and, yes, you, you've got to get them hope."

Hope would be the central message of Milk's speeches over the next seventeen months. He would be a spokesperson for neighborhoods, unions, and minorities, and gay rights certainly would be at the top of his agenda. But with gays now embattled in a culture war, with large numbers of homosexuals exalting him as a leader and hero of the gay movement, Milk seemed to embrace a higher calling.

Milk would speak for the thousands of gay Americans who lived in a dark, secret world; who were made to feel sinful and abnormal; who despaired to the point where suicide seemed like the best way out.

Milk had lived in the closet for much of his life, but after breaking out he felt freer and more alive than ever before. Now, emboldened by the aggression of the anti-gay crusades, Milk would urge others to come out and to join the openly gay community.

Harvey Milk was on the verge of becoming a major political figure—and one of the most influential human-rights leaders the country had ever seen.

6

THE HISTORIC ELECTION

Tory Hartmann, a veteran campaign worker for the Democratic Party, walked into Castro Camera in 1977 and couldn't believe her eyes.

"That campaign was anything but normal," Hartmann said. "One day I was in the campaign headquarters, and I was looking around at this motley group of people. It was a lot of fun, but give me a break!"

Working the desk in a dark corner, where the light on the phone was the brightest illumination, was Anne Kronenberg, Milk's twenty-three-year-old campaign manager. A lesbian with bushy blond hair, Kronenberg often dressed in biker clothes: blue jeans with a leather jacket. She was playing the lead role in helping Milk get elected to San Francisco's Board of Supervisors.

Hartmann scanned the room. "I looked at Anne . . . with the motorcycle clothes on," Hartmann said. "And then there's John with his three-piece suit, and there's little Michael Wong, who Milk always called his lotus blossom. And a couple of old ladies who would be in there too, bless their hearts. And the silk screening on the side, and you'd smell the ink—you know, all this hubbub. And he's trying to run a business in the front. Everything happened in this long, dingy camera store. Everything from 'Save the Whales' to get elected."

After losing his three previous campaigns for public office, Milk ran this one the same way—haphazardly, with the support of local volunteers. Nearly broke, Milk did much of the pavement-pounding himself. He visited shops,

Harvey Milk

(Courtesy of AP Images)

knocked on doors, and shook hands on the busy streets during morning and evening rush hours. The human billboards returned, all lined up on city blocks with their "Harvey Milk Supervisor" signs.

Most of the time, especially in front of the cameras, Milk effused charm and charisma. He talked energetically and engaged people with his warm, welcoming smile. But Milk overextended himself, and no one wanted to be around him when he became tired and cranky.

Kronenberg cherished her friendship with Milk, but, she said, "he was a very difficult person to work with. He did have temper fits, where he would be just like a little kid sometimes, for no good reason except that he was probably exhausted."

In the newly formed District 5, Milk was the front-runner among seventeen candidates, about half of whom were gay. Gay lawyer Rick Stokes was among the favorites. Stokes had endured the hell of electroshock therapy, a cruel and useless procedure. Believing that homosexuality was a mental disorder, some psychiatrists in earlier years had ordered electrical jolts to the brain, believing that it might make the brain return to "normal." Despite being coerced into this horrific procedure, Stokes disavowed confrontational politics in favor of working within the system. He was supported by the Alice B. Toklas Memorial Democratic Club, the moderate gay organization.

In the largely gay district, only liberal candidates had a chance of winning. But, said Milk, "we don't want sympathetic liberals, we want gays to represent gays. I represent the gay street people—the fourteen-year-old runaway from San Antonio. We have to make up for hundreds of years of persecution. We have to give hope to that poor runaway kid from San Antonio. They go to the bars because churches are hostile. They need hope! They need a piece of the pie!"

Though Milk was the favorite in the race, it would be a tough road to victory. Mayor George Moscone threw his weight behind Stokes, and other political leaders supported liberal candidate Terrance Hallinan. Campaigning day and night took its toll on Milk, whose forty-seven-year-old body was succumbing to exhaustion. Moreover, he began to receive death threats from those who didn't want gays taking power in their city and country.

Milk would receive death threats the rest of his life, but they wouldn't hold him back. For much of his life, Milk had felt that he wouldn't live a long life—that for whatever reason he would die in middle age. Once he became a major political figure, he talked about the strong possibility that he would be assassinated. Yet he forged ahead, refusing to be spooked into submission.

One day during the campaign, the threats became all too real. Someone set off powerful fireworks that shattered Castro Camera's windows as well as those of three other stores on the street. The news made the front page of the next day's *San Francisco Chronicle*. Most likely, the attack strengthened the resolve of the Castro community. The gays of Castro, who numbered as many as 30,000, would come out in force on election day, November 8, and vote for Milk for supervisor of District 5.

A three-time loser, Milk fretted during the big day, fearing another defeat. But this time he didn't have to worry. Milk tallied 30.5 percent of the vote, more than double the individual totals of Stokes and Hallinan. No openly gay politician had ever been elected to such a high position in California. Milk was on Cloud 9.

"The victory will give hope to minorities, hope to the disenfranchised and to the people who always felt that the government didn't work," Milk said. "They'll feel that if a gay can do it, they can do it."

For the man who had always been searching for a stage, this was an ultimate experience. Milk boasted that gays throughout America would be watching him as a potential role model, "and I'll be it," he said.

The victory celebration in the Castro had a fairytale feel. A huge crowd gathered around Castro Camera, and the lights of television crews illuminated the sidewalk. Finally, the man of the hour arrived. Two motorcycles, one driven by Kronenberg and the other by her partner, pulled up, with Milk seated on the rear of the partner's bike. When he climbed off, he flashed a huge smile and opened his arms.

Photos from that historic evening show gay men of all ethnicities crowded together and smiling jubilantly. This was a victory not just for Milk, but for gays and lesbians everywhere. Milk partied at a jam-packed Castro bar, and at one point he doused himself with champagne. In interviews, he said he would prove that even though he was gay, he would be concerned with everyone's needs.

"This is similar to when [John F.] Kennedy was elected," Milk said, referring to the first Catholic president. "People thought the pope would run the country. But after six months in office, when he started doing things, people never questioned him again. If I do a good job, after a while people won't care if I'm green or with three heads."

The days following the election were filled with elation and grim foreboding. On the morning after, Milk and his supporters gathered on the busy Market Street hoisting signs that said "Thank You." People shook Milk's hand and honked their horns in support. In the upcoming days, letters came in from all over the city and country. Most congratulated Milk and thanked him for breaking political barriers and making them proud to be gay. Other letters, however, threatened his life.

Following the election, Milk was asked to appear on talk shows with Dan White, another newly elected supervisor who opposed gay rights.

(Left and above) Harvey Milk celebrates in his camera store his
election as a San Francisco supervisor on election night, November 8, 1977.
(Courtesy of Robert Clay / Alamy)

A former soldier during the Vietnam War, White served San Francisco as a police officer and fire fighter. "If he had been a breakfast cereal," said an acquaintance of White, "he would have had to be Wheaties."

On the talk shows, Milk and White talked kindly about each other. But while confiding with his friend Dennis Seely, Milk shared his true feelings. "Dan White is just stupid . . . ," Milk said, "been brought up with all those prejudices."

Seely said that White was bad news, that he was just like all the other police officers in the city—that he would be anti-gay throughout his term in office.

Milk disagreed. "As the years pass, the guy can be educated," Milk told Seely. "Everyone can be reached. Everyone can be educated and helped. You think some people are hopeless—not me."

On inauguration day, Milk wanted to make a splash. He asked that the ceremonies be held outside city hall instead of inside the building because all of his supporters couldn't fit inside. Milk, with his arm around another man, walked to the inauguration that day, followed by more than a hundred of his friends and supporters. While other supervisors introduced their husbands and wives, Milk showed off Jack Lira, whom he referred to as his lover and partner. Milk was making it clear that gays would play a visible, vocal role in San Francisco politics.

Milk wasn't the only minority inaugurated to the Board of Supervisors that day. Gordon Lau, representing the Chinatown district, became the first Chinese American supervisor—a momentous occasion considering that the city had boasted a large Chinese population since the gold rush. In addition, the first African American woman, Ella Hill Hutch, and the first feminist and unwed mother, Carol Ruth Silver, were sworn in, and a Latino supervisor joined the Board of Supervisors.

But Milk was the one who grabbed the headlines. That afternoon, he proposed that the board pass legislation to eliminate all forms of discrimination against homosexuals. Then, after the supervisors elected Dianne Feinstein board president by a 6-5 vote, Milk proved to be a thorn in the board's side. The other supervisors wanted to make the vote unanimous as a show of solidarity, but Milk—who had voted for Lau as president—refused. Milk sent the message that he wouldn't be a cog in the machine; instead, he would remain a maverick who stood up for what he believed in.

Early in his term, Milk laid down the law with Mayor Moscone. Milk insisted that the mayor become more proactive on behalf of the gay community. Moreover, if Moscone were to appoint a homosexual to a position, he would have to clear that person with Milk first. Milk did not want the Alice B. Toklas Democratic Club, which Milk felt was too acquiescent, to be the strongest voice for gays in San Francisco. Instead, Milk wanted that role.

Harvey Milk's inaugural walk to city hall from the Castro neighborhood, January 9, 1978. *(Courtesy of Dan Nicoletta)*

Despite Milk's forceful behavior, Moscone was willing to adhere to his requests. Milk did, after all, have plenty of clout; one in five people in San Francisco was gay. Milk and Moscone would be close allies in their remaining months.

While the board moved forward on Milk's proposed gay-rights legislation, Milk voiced his opinions on a variety of matters. He called for a tax on the several hundred thousand commuters who drove into the city each day. He railed against the proposed parking garage that would be built next to city hall. The construction would mean that sixty-seven housing units would have to be torn down. Milk said it was outrageous to give more priorities to cars than to people's homes.

Milk had long favored the rights of residents over corporate developers, and as supervisor he took a stand. On multiple occasions, he voiced his opposition to development projects, including new housing construction in the Castro. Milk worried that home prices were becoming too high, and that more new, high-priced homes would make the area unaffordable for minorities.

Milk worked wonders on behalf of District 5. He successfully fought to keep open a local library branch and an elementary school. For safety reasons, he was able to get dozens of stop signs in his district, and he pushed to fix the many potholes in the area.

As he did during his years on Wall Street, Milk both amused and irritated his fellow workers with his biting jokes and strong opinions. He talked frequently with Dan White, whom Milk said was "basically a decent person, just uneducated. He'll learn."

At first, Milk supported White on an initiative that was important to the conservative supervisor. White opposed the transformation of an empty convent in his district into a mental health facility. Though he initially sided with White, Milk changed his mind when he learned that the facility would allow its residents to be close to their families. The board voted 6-5 to allow the convent to be converted to the new facility.

It was a major blow to White, and he blamed Milk. Thereafter, White held a grudge and opposed all of Milk's initiatives.

Unfazed by his rival, Milk forged ahead. During a political speech in San Diego on March 10, Milk delivered one of his famous "Hope" speeches. The long oration concluded with the following words:

> The young gay people in the Altoona, Pennsylvanias and the Richmond, Minnesotas who are coming out and hear Anita Bryant on television and her story, the only thing they have to look forward to is hope. And you have to give them hope. Hope for a better world, hope for a better tomorrow, hope for a better place to come to if the pressures at home are too great. Hope that all will be all right. Without hope, not only gays, but the blacks, the seniors, the handicapped, the us'es, the us'es will give up . . . So if there is a message I have to give, it is that if I have found one overriding thing about my personal election, it's the fact that if a gay person can be elected, it's a green light. And you and you and you, you have to give people hope.

On March 20, Milk achieved his greatest success as a legislator when the Board of Supervisors passed a gay-rights ordinance in San Francisco. By a vote of 10-1, with only Dan White opposing, they created the most stringent pro-gay legislation in the country. The new ordinance would ban discrimination in housing, employment, and public accommodation.

"This one has teeth," Milk told reporters. "A person can go to court if his rights are violated once this is passed."

Mayor Moscone would sign the bill, and even a police union spokesman stated that the San Francisco Police Department did not oppose the ordinance. White, though, voiced his objections. He said that private businesses and private schools that were morally opposed to homosexuality should not be forced to hire gays and lesbians.

"I respect the private rights of all people, including gays," White said. But he added: "According to the city attorney's office, if a transvestite shows up at a private school with all the qualifications for teaching, they cannot refuse to hire him for an [open position] even if they object to having a man dressed as a woman in their school."

The passage of the bill only deepened the division between Milk and White. Milk's needling, which had annoyed co-workers at his previous jobs, didn't sit well with the straight-laced supervisor. In a discussion about homosexuality, Milk told White, "Don't knock it unless you've tried it."

Besides the historic gay-rights legislation, Milk was responsible for only one other bill during his tenure as supervisor. It was called the "pooper scooper law." Milk insisted that San Francisco residents pick up their dogs' feces. The law was in line with Milk's belief that residents should take care of their neighborhoods. But more than that, he also felt that it would garner him publicity.

Sure enough, Milk and the doggy doo-doo became a human-interest story all over the country. Milk added drama to the tale when he invited reporters to Duboce Park and "accidentally" stepped in dog poop. In reality, he had spotted the excrement before the cameras had arrived and staged the messy incident.

Milk loved the attention—not just because he had a big ego, but because he thought it would further the gay cause. "All over the country, they're reading about me," Milk said in regard to the pooper scooper law, "and the story doesn't center on me being gay. It's just about a gay person who is doing his job."

While Milk delighted in his new job, troubles loomed at home. During his 1977 campaign, he had met Jack Lira, a Mexican American in his mid-twenties. Disowned by his father because he was gay, Lira fled to San Francisco, where he lived with a wealthy gay man before moving in with Milk. Lira drank heavily, was prone to severe depression, and lacked employable skills.

Milk and Lira broke up, but on one fateful day afterward Lira entered Milk's apartment while the supervisor was at work. When Milk opened his apartment door at 7 p.m., he spotted an unsettling trail of papers and beer cans leading to the enclosed back porch. Pulling back a black curtain, he saw Lira hanging from a rope.

"You've always loved the circus, Milk," stated a note pinned to the curtain. "What do you think of my last act?"

Lira had known that Milk was seeing another man, and hanging himself in Milk's apartment was, in part, retribution. Milk was forced to deal with the horrible aftermath. He grabbed a kitchen knife and sliced the rope, then ran to the nearby fire department. Fire fighters rushed in and pronounced that Lira was deceased.

Meanwhile, Milk found Lira's handwritten notes all over his apartment—in drawers, books, and clothes. Some were mean criticisms of Milk, while others attacked the recent anti-gay crusades.

Undoubtedly, Lira wanted his lover to share the pain that he had endured, and certainly Milk was shaken and saddened. Milk's friends wondered if he would be ridden with guilt. Not only had Milk broken up with Lira, but Lira had called him earlier in the day saying that he needed to talk to him. Moreover, the coroner estimated that Lira had hanged himself at 6:15—the time Milk normally came home. Had he left at his usual time, or a few minutes earlier, he might have prevented the gruesome tragedy. However, Lira's sister convinced Milk that he actually had been a good influence on her brother. Lira, in fact, had attempted suicide multiple times before he had ever met Milk.

Death seemed to loom over Milk at every turn of his life. The passage of the gay-rights ordinance prompted many people to pen hostile letters. Anne Kronenberg felt troubled as she read through the hate mail, and she feared that Milk would be gunned down during the Gay Freedom Day Parade in June 1978. Milk was so aware that he could be assassinated that he had come to accept it. His attitude was: If it happens, it happens. He refused to give in.

Outside of his legislative duties, Milk waged a greater battle in 1978. California senator John Briggs, spurred by the success of the anti-gay campaigns, launched the Briggs Initiative. The senator wanted to pass legislation that would force schools to deny employment to gay teachers and perhaps even those who supported gay rights. Briggs, who was running for governor that year, believed he could use this popular platform to win election.

In his pronouncements and literature, Briggs viciously maligned homosexuals, using the same tactics that Save Our Children had used. His staff helped get the measure on the ballot for the November 1978 elections. It would be called Proposition 6.

"What Proposition 6 is really all about is the right of parents to determine who will be teaching their children," Briggs said. "We don't allow people who believe in practicing bestiality to teach our children. We don't let prostitutes teach our children. And the reason we don't is because it is illegal to be a prostitute. But it is not illegal to be a homosexual in California."

When news of the Briggs Initiative first arose, all eyes turned to Harvey Milk. And the supervisor from San Francisco came out fighting. While Briggs traveled throughout California to discuss Proposition 6, so did Milk. When Briggs hosted an event, Milk was there, defending gays and speaking against the initiative.

"There are already laws on the books to protect our children," Milk said during a joint press conference with Briggs. "Everybody from . . . [California Governor] Jerry Brown to newspaper editors across the state agree that indeed we have the laws to protect our children."

Milk denounced the charge that gay teachers were not the right role models for children. "I was born of heterosexual parents," he said. "I was taught by heterosexual teachers in a fiercely heterosexual society, with television ads and newspaper ads fiercely heterosexual, a society that puts down homosexuality. And why am I homosexual if I'm affected by role models? . . . No offense meant, but if teachers are going to affect you as role model, there'd be a lot of nuns running around the streets today."

Milk and lesbian Sally Gearhart, a speech professor at San Francisco State University, together chaired the United Fund to Defeat the Briggs Initiative. One of their goals was to explode the myth that gay men were prone to molest boys—a seed that the Briggs campaign had planted in its literature. Briggs himself denied making the claim. But in a televised debate, Milk confronted Briggs, waving the literature and flustering the senator:

Harvey Milk listens as Senator John Briggs, the author of Prop. 6, the anti-gay teacher initiative, is interviewed by newsmen a block from San Francisco's famed Polk Street, on November 1, 1978. Briggs, under tight police security, was kept a block away at Larkin and Sutter streets.
(Courtesy of AP Images Photo/Sal Veder)

Milk: You yourself say that the heterosexual is the child molester . . . . If child molestation is not an issue, why do you put out literature that hammers it home? Why do you play on that myth and fear?

Briggs: Same thing with V.D. [venereal disease], Harvey. We put out publications about V.D. so you can avoid it.

Milk (raising the literature): This is campaign literature.

Briggs: Yes, we're trying to keep people from falling into that trap. We're trying to prevent it by pointing it out. And by the way, I don't make the statement that 95 percent of [molestations are committed by] heterosexuals . . .

Milk: What percent is it?

Harvey Milk, left, talks with Gwenn Craig and Bill Kraus, co-cordinators of the
San Francisco "No on Prop 6" program in San Francisco, on November 7, 1978.
(Courtesy of AP Images Photo/Sal Veder)

Briggs: I don't know—you tell me.

Milk: The state says 90 to 95 percent.

Briggs: Well, I've never seen that in writing. I don't make those statements—you do . . . . We are not talking about child molestation. The fact is, at least 95 percent of the people are heterosexual. If we took heterosexuals out and homosexuals out, you know what?

Milk: We'd have no teachers.

Briggs: We'd have no teachers.

Milk: No child molestation. So you're saying that the percentage of population is equal to the percentage of child molestation. There's no difference.

Briggs: No, I'm not saying that at all.

Milk: But that's what you just said!

Briggs: No, I'm saying that we cannot prevent child molestation, so let's cut our odds down and take out the homosexual group and keep the heterosexual group. . .

At that, Milk threw up his hands in a fit of laughter. Gearhart picked up the debate from there.

Gearhart: Why take out the homosexual group when overwhelmingly it is true that it is the heterosexual men, I might add, who are the child molesters?

Briggs: I believe that's a myth. I've never seen those figures.

Gearhart: Oh, Senator!

Gearhart went on to state that the FBI, the National Council on Family Relations, the Santa Clara County Child Sexual Abuse Treatment Center, and other organizations had found that gay men were no more likely to molest children then a straight men.

Milk's well-executed efforts to defeat the Briggs Initiative earned him much publicity and praise throughout California. Nevertheless, it looked for a long time that he was fighting a losing battle. In late August 1978, opinion polls showed that Californians—by more than a 2-1 margin—would side with Briggs and vote yes on Proposition 6. In fact, Briggs had such an overwhelming advantage that some gays thought that even most San Franciscans would vote yes.

But thanks to Milk's public showdowns with Briggs and canvassing by volunteers, the tide began to change. More and more, Californians realized that pedophilia among homosexuals was a myth and that the initiative was an infringement on civil liberties.

Always thinking big, Milk sought to elicit the support of President Jimmy Carter. Though he was generally liberal on issues of social justice, Carter had been reluctant to voice his support for gay-rights legislation. At an outdoor rally in Los Angeles, Milk—at the top of his voice and punching the air for emphasis—demanded that the president get involved.

"Join me in this message," Milk urged. "Jimmy Carter, listen to us. You want to lead? You want to be the world's leader in human rights? Well, damn it, lead! There are fifteen million lesbians and gay men waiting to hear your voice!"

Throughout September, the grassroots effort to defeat Prop 6 made tremendous strides. A poll taken late in the month revealed that nearly as many citizens were against the proposal as those who favored it. Even former California governor Ronald Reagan, the famed conservative, opposed the measure. "Whatever else it is, homosexuality is not a contagious disease like the measles," Reagan stated. "Prevailing scientific opinion is that an individual's sexuality is determined at a very early age and that a child's teachers do not really influence this."

California governor Jerry Brown, a strong liberal, also opposed Prop 6. With Brown running for reelection in 1978, Carter stopped at the state capital in Sacramento to show his support for the incumbent. Carter was ready to step off the stage at an outdoor rally when Brown said something to him. The remark was meant to be candid, but the nearby microphones picked up his words. Said Brown to Carter: "[Former president Gerald] Ford and Reagan have both come out against it, so I think you're perfectly safe."

With that, the president returned to the microphone and said, "Also, I want to ask everybody to vote against Proposition 6."

In just a few weeks' time, opinions about the Briggs Initiative and gays in general changed dramatically in California. On November 7, statewide voters defeated Proposition 6 by the surprisingly large margin of 59 percent to 41 percent. Gays throughout the state were ecstatic. Not only would gay and lesbians be accepted as teachers, but the activists had reversed the momentum when it came to gay rights.

The greatest celebrations were in San Francisco. Gwenn Craig, co-chair of the local anti-Prop 6 effort, joined others in blowing up balloons at a local bar. "We were elated," Craig said. San Francisco's gay marching band entered the bar, belting out tunes.

At another location, Milk—the inspirational leader of the anti-Prop 6 campaign—climbed a platform and addressed a joyous, raucous crowd:

> [S]o far, a lot of people have joined us and rejected
> Proposition 6, and we owe them something. We owe them
> to continue the education campaign that took place. We
> must destroy the myths once and for all—shatter them. We
> must continue to speak out. And most importantly, most

importantly, every gay person must come out. As difficult as it is, you must tell your immediate family. You must tell your relatives. You must tell your friends if indeed they are your friends. You must tell your neighbors. You must tell the people in the stores you shop in. . . . And once they realize that we are indeed their children, and that we are indeed everywhere, every myth, every lie, every innuendo will be destroyed once and for all. And once you do, you will feel so much better.

Milk left the podium amid thunderous howls of joy. Men and women beamed, arms raised in triumph and freedom.

Over the previous years, gays and lesbians of San Francisco had made great progress. The Castro community had grown and become identified with the gay rights movement across the world. The success of the Castro Village Association, the overwhelming turnouts at the 1977 and '78 Gay Freedom Day Parades, the first elected openly gay official, the passage of the gay-rights legislation, and now the historic defeat of Proposition 6 had advanced the cause. In each instance, one man stood at the center of it all: Harvey Milk.

Milk had directly improved the lives of San Francisco's gays and lesbians. His work on Prop 6 helped save gay teachers from being fired. The gay-rights legislation helped others live normal lives. And his inspirational speeches made homosexuals feel proud and self-confident.

"You could just see that people stood a little taller," said Walter Caplan, a friend of Milk.

In November 1978, Milk stood at the pinnacle of his career. And yet, in the back of his mind, he feared that he was doomed—that a gay-hating bigot would fire a shot at him, and there would be no Bill Sipple to save him. Other political leaders had been assassinated in the previous fifteen years—John F. Kennedy, Martin Luther King, and Robert Kennedy—and two people had tried to kill President Ford. Milk's fears were not unwarranted.

Milk was so preoccupied with his own death that he made three audiotapes that served as political wills. The tapes were made for his attorney, John Wahl, and his close friends, Caplan and Frank Robinson. Should he be assassinated, Milk said in the tapes, he wanted Mayor Moscone to appoint Robinson as his replacement.

Each tape was a little different than the others. On the tape for Robinson, he uttered the immortal line "If a bullet should enter my brain, let that bullet destroy every closet door."

On November 18, he made a tape for Caplan. On that tape, Milk discussed who he did not want to replace him on the board, including gay moderates Jim Foster and Rick Stokes. "[T]hose people never understood the movement," he said. Besides his top pick, Robinson, Milk listed three others who could replace him, including Anne Kronenberg.

In the Caplan tape, Milk called John Briggs "an evil man" and accused Anita Bryant of "playing gymnastics with the Bible"—meaning interpreting the book to suit her own agenda. Milk concluded the tape by explaining what the gay-rights movement was all about. "It's not about personal gain, not about ego, not about power," he said. "It's about giving those young people out there in the Altoona, Pennsylvanias hope. You got to give them hope."

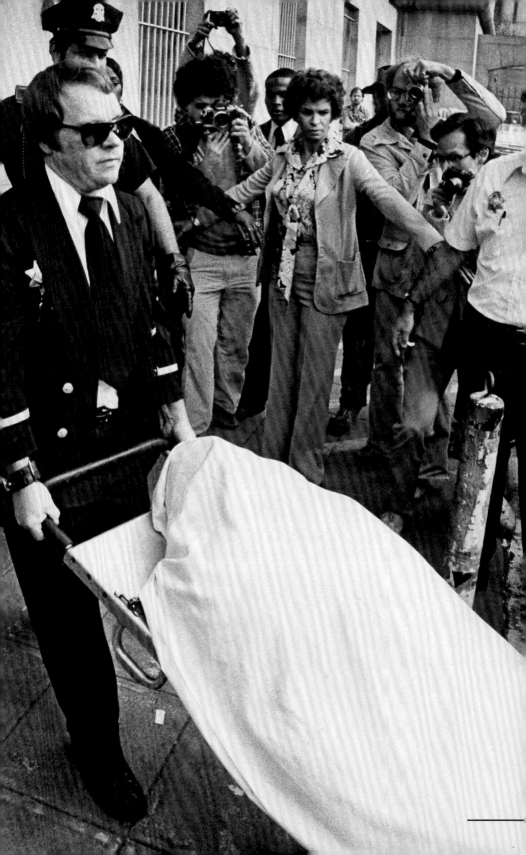

KILLED IN COLD BLOOD

7

Dan White was a heroic figure to the conservatives of San Francisco. After all, here was a clean-cut, church-going young man who had served his country in Vietnam and protected his community as a police officer and fire fighter. He was the board supervisor who had stood up for traditional morals and values.

White even made personal sacrifices to serve his people. Because his city hall job was technically considered a part-time position, he earned a paltry salary of $9,600. In 1978, after his wife, Mary Ann, had to quit her teaching job because she was pregnant, the Whites struggled to make ends meet. They tried opening a fried-potato stand near the waterfront, but White's supervisor duties consumed too much of his time. On November 10, 1978, White decided to resign from the board.

The resignation sent shockwaves through city hall. Six of the eleven board members had been conservative. With White gone, liberal Mayor George Moscone had the authority to appoint his replacement, which undoubtedly would have been a liberal. Though Moscone said he was "really sorry to see [White] go" and "I think he's a good guy," Milk and the other progressive supervisors were elated that White was leaving.

Meanwhile, conservative groups and city developers panicked when they heard the news—fearing that a liberal-dominated board would quash their agendas. The Police Officers Association and the Board of Realtors pressured White to change his mind. They would help him finan-

Police remove a body from San Francisco city hall.

(Courtesy of AP Images)

cially, but for goodness sake he had to get back on the board. White relented, and he asked Moscone to rescind his resignation.

Moscone reportedly planned to give him his job back until Milk entered the equation. Milk was adamant that Moscone appoint a liberal replacement. He even threatened the mayor, telling him that he would have a hard time getting reelected in 1979 if he and the city's gay population didn't support him.

Moscone said that he would announce his decision about White on Monday, November 27.

The week leading up to that fateful day was marked by the Jonestown massacre, a horrific chapter in San Francisco's history. In 1977 and 1978, Reverend Jim Jones and a thousand members of his Peoples Temple cult had moved from their San Francisco headquarters and began to build a town they called Jonestown in Guyana, a poor country on the northern coast of South America. Jones ostensibly wanted to create a socialist utopia for his poor, mostly African American flock. Yet he was also eager to escape the media, who were beginning to investigate what was going on inside his cult.

Back in 1975, Temple followers had assisted the campaigns of Harvey Milk and George Moscone. After Moscone was elected mayor, he returned the favor by naming Jones the chairman of the San Francisco Housing Authority Commission. Jones became a seemingly legitimate politician, securing multiple meetings with Vice President Walter Mondale. Yet Temple life was anything but normal, and once Jones joined his followers in Jonestown in the summer of 1977, conditions there deteriorated.

The members lived a communal lifestyle, working long hours in primitive conditions. Through speeches that blared constantly through the loudspeakers, Jones railed against the evils of American capitalism and trumpeted the virtues of Soviet, Cuban, and North Korean communism. Jones used armed guards and drugs to prevent people from escaping. Children who misbehaved were lowered into a "torture hole" (a well) as punishment.

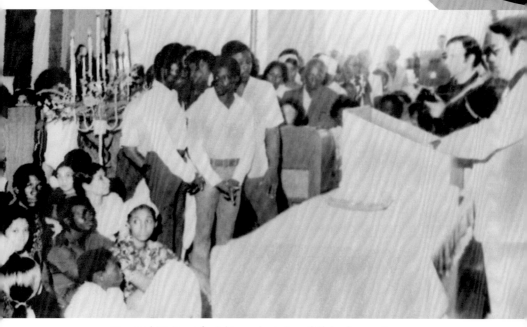

Reverend Jim Jones, far right, speaks during a faith healing service on November 20, 1978, in Jonestown, Guyana. *(Courtesy of AP Images)*

On February 18, 1978, the *San Francisco Examiner* wrote a story condemning Jones's treatment of his people. Milk responded by writing to President Carter. In a letter dated February 19, 1978, on official city and county of San Francisco stationery, Milk defended the reverend. He wrote: "Rev. Jones is widely known in the minority communities here and elsewhere as a man of the highest character, who has undertaken constructive remedies for social problems which have been amazing in their scope and effectiveness."

Had Milk been aware of the alarming conditions in Jonestown, he might not have written such a letter. Nevertheless, the letter will forever be a blemish on Milk's legacy.

As 1978 progressed, Jones feared that U.S. forces would travel to Guyana and shut down Jonestown. The reverend had his people prepare for such a day of reckoning: they would rebel through mass suicide. On more than one occasion, the residents practiced a suicide drill in which they lined up and drank red liquid. If the fateful day came, the liquid would contain deadly poison.

Such a time arrived in the fall of 1978. On November 17, U.S. Congressman Leo Ryan of California led a contingent of government officials, journalists, and relatives of Temple members to Guyana. Ryan and a few others (but no reporters) were allowed into the community, where the hosts put on a good face.

The guests stayed overnight in Jonestown, but the next day chaos ensued. Fourteen Temple defectors left with the Ryan contingent. As the group was about to leave on two airplanes, Jones's Red Brigade security force arrived and opened fire on one of the planes. Ryan, NBC reporter Don Harris, and three others were killed.

Upon hearing the news of the murders, Jones realized that government officials would storm into Jonestown and shut it down. He urged his people to commit revolutionary suicide, and they obeyed. More than nine hundred people lined up to drink poisoned Flavor Aid, and each died just minutes later. Excluding natural disasters, it was the greatest loss of American civilians in history.

News of the tragedy sickened Americans, especially those in the Bay Area, where most of the victims were from. "I proceeded to vomit and cry," Moscone said. Many wondered about the mayor's involvement, since he and Jones and been strong political allies. "I'm not taking any responsibility," Moscone said. "It's not mine to shoulder."

Little is known about Milk's reaction to the tragedy, although he must have wondered about the letter he wrote to the president. If that were made public, it could have been politically devastating for him.

On the morning of Monday, November 27, Moscone and Milk went to work at city hall. Hearts were still heavy, and security was heightened amid rumors that Jones had hired hit squads to enact revenge on political enemies. That morning, the mayor was scheduled to announce his

Opposite Page: Bodies lie in Jim Jones's Peoples Temple after the cult's mass suicide in Jonestown, Guyana, November 1978. Jones and more than nine hundred of his followers died in the compound. *(Courtesy of AP Images)*

decision about the supervisor position at 11:30. He knew who he wanted for the position, and it wasn't Dan White.

Moscone, in fact, had told colleagues days earlier that White would not be allowed back. White was incensed when he heard the news, and on Monday morning he intended to confront the mayor—with a gun.

White knew he couldn't walk through the metal detectors of city hall while carrying a weapon, so he devised an elaborate scheme. That morning, an unidentified woman picked up White at his home and drove him to city hall. Next to a parking ramp, White knocked on a basement window, which a man opened for him. White told him that he had forgotten his keys to the door that the supervisors typically entered after parking their cars. Recognizing White, the man let him in through the window.

White made his way to the reception area of the mayor's office. Moscone came out and greeted him with a smile, although secretary Cyr Copertini and press aide Mel Wax were nervous to see the disgruntled former supervisor. The man who Moscone was about to name as the new supervisor, Don Horanzy, was in the reception area. "I was worried," Wax said, "that [Horanzy] and White would see each other and we'd have a scene."

Moscone and White agreed to talk. The mayor led his visitor into the formal office and then into a sitting room, where they could be more comfortable. Copertini wasn't crazy about the two men being alone, but when she asked Moscone if he'd like someone to sit in with them, he laughed her off.

Shortly after the meeting began, Copertini heard several sharp noises. Deputy Mayor Rudy Nothenberg entered the office and saw Moscone bleeding heavily. "It was awful," Nothenberg said. "It was shock and panic. You don't know what you can do for him. You scream for the cops, which is what I did."

White, meanwhile, had bolted from the scene, only to turn up on the other side of the building at the suite of supervisor offices. He raced past Dianne Feinstein's office and into Milk's office. "Harvey, can I see you a minute?" he asked. He then led Milk into his old office.

White wasted no time. He drew his revolver and pulled the trigger. "Oh, no," Milk cried after the bullet entered his body. White kept firing: two more shots to his torso, which might not have killed him, followed by two fatal shots to the head.

Carl Carlson, a friend of Milk, saw White leave the bloody office and shut the door. There was absolutely no doubt that Dan White had just murdered Harvey Milk.

Feinstein, realizing what had just happened, walked in a daze into the office. "I put my finger to see if there was any pulse," she remembered years later, "and it went in a bullet hole in his chest."

White ran to Denise Apcar, his former aide, and demanded that she give him her car keys. She relented, and White fled toward an exit. "He was a wild man—he was just a wild man," one witness said.

White drove a few blocks and stopped at a fast-food restaurant. He called his wife, Mary Ann, asking her to meet him at St. Mary's

Cathedral. She arrived quickly via taxi and saw her husband in the chapel. White told her that he had killed the mayor and Milk. After talking for a few minutes, the couple walked to the police station where White had once worked.

Dan White, left, is taken into custody by Police Department Inspector Howard Bailey in the basement of the Hall of Justice in San Francisco. (*Courtesy of John Storey/San Francisco Chronicle/Corbis*)

Meanwhile, police and reporters raced to city hall. Amid the chaos, few knew exactly what had happened. Had the mayor been killed, or Milk? Many thought that Jim Jones's supporters were involved.

Feinstein, her eyes glazed, supported by police chief Charles Gain, addressed the horde of reporters. "As president of the Board of Supervisors," Feinstein said, "it is my duty to inform you that both Mayor Moscone and Supervisor Harvey Milk have been shot and killed." Those in attendance gasped. "The suspect," Feinstein added, "is Supervisor Dan White."

Feinstein, who had lost her bid for mayor three years earlier, had now—on the worst day of her life—become the acting mayor. Over the next hour, the police gathered evidence while placing Milk's remains in a body bag. Cleve Jones, a friend of Milk who would become a world-famous activist, arrived at the scene with Scott Smith, Milk's former partner.

Feinstein's pronouncement was repeated on TV and radio throughout the day. Moscone's wife heard the news on a car radio, while her four children learned of their father's murder while at school. Joe Campbell, Milk's longtime partner, was told of the deaths by a hitchhiker, then broke into tears.

San Franciscans were in a state of shock. Just a week after the tragic news from Guyana, they lost their mayor—a native son. The pain of the gay community was even more intense; Moscone had been their first "friend" in the mayor's office, and Harvey Milk was their beloved leader and champion—the man who had fought for them like no one else ever had. Now, like that, they were gone.

President Jimmy Carter released a public statement that afternoon. He referred to Milk as a "hard-working and dedicated supervisor, a leader of San Francisco's gay community, who kept his promise to represent all constituents."

Some mourners walked to city hall and placed flowers on the steps. One angry man added a small sign that said, "Are you happy, Anita?" In the Castro district, mourners closed their stores and others gathered in the streets, particularly at the corner of Castro and 18th Street.

Word spread that a candlelight vigil would be held that evening at Market and Castro streets. Needing to grieve, and finding comfort in numbers, men and women poured out of their homes to join the vigil. Many purchased candles, which they held in paper cups. The crowd swelled so large that they had no choice but to move forward. The vigil turned into a march, as they walked toward downtown.

It was an experience that no one would forget. They marched in silence, in unity, the light of the candles guiding their way. As they reached the Civic Center, many placed their candles around the statue of Abraham Lincoln. Those in the enormous crowd, estimated at 30,000 to 40,000, maintained their composure, excluding the sobs and tears. Much to the crowd's disbelief, Joan Baez—the famed folk singer and a voice of the counterculture in the 1960s—arrived at the scene and led the marchers in "Kumbaya," "Amazing Grace," and "Oh, Freedom."

A passerby left flowers and the afternoon headlines on
the steps of city hall in San Francisco, November 28, 1978.
(Courtesy of San Francisco Public Library)

More than 25,000 persons jammed the park and streets around San Francisco's city hall on Monday, November 28, 1978, in a spontaneous demonstration of grief for slain Mayor George Moscone and Supervisor Harvey Milk. *(Courtesy of AP Images)*

On the day after the murder, the *San Francisco Examiner* ran a black band at the top of its front page—"A City in Agony," it read—and flags were flown at half-mast throughout California. That day, Milk's supporters began their quest to honor the fallen leader. After the mayor's staff decided that Moscone's body would lie in state beneath the city hall rotunda, Milk's aides insisted that his body lie in state there as well. And that night, members of the San Francisco Gay Democratic Club voted to change the organization's name to the Harvey Milk Gay Democratic Club. The vote was unanimous.

On Wednesday, a memorial service was staged on city hall's front stairs. Acting Mayor Feinstein spoke for the city when she said, "The murders of Mayor George Moscone and Supervisor Harvey Milk shake and pain us all. In the wake of the tragedies in Guyana, this additional senseless monstrosity seems simply unreal. . . . In our sorrow, this lovely jewel of a city seems a dark and saddened place."

Also on Wednesday, Temple Emmanue-El held a service for Milk, who had never strongly embraced religion. That night, Milk's brother, Robert, arrived at the airport. Reporters had many questions for the only living member of Milk's immediate family.

While a large funeral for George Moscone was held at St. Mary's Cathedral on Thursday, Milk was remembered at the San Francisco War Memorial Opera House. Planners deemed it appropriate, for Milk had loved opera since the days of his youth. Several thousand people attended, and hundreds more gathered outside. Governor Jerry Brown was there, and others eulogized the fallen leader. Anne Kronenberg, one of the speakers, read a poem that Milk had written just a few weeks earlier:

I can be killed with ease.
I can be cut right down.
But I cannot fall back into my closet.
I have grown.
I am not myself.
I am too many.
I am all of us.

Though Harvey Milk served only eleven months on the San Francisco Board of Supervisors, his public role inspired many to champion equal rights for gays and lesbians. In October 2009, California governor Arnold Schwarzenegger signed into law a bill that establishes May 22, Milk's birthday, as a day recognizing the slain civil rights leader. The day will not be a public holiday in the state, but will be marked by public schools.
(Courtesy of San Francisco Public Library)

Though normally soft-spoken, Kronenberg paid homage to Milk by raising her fist and shouting: "He knew that our time would come. And our time is now!" The people rose to their feet and cheered—just like during Milk's many inspirational speeches.

No one, it seemed, was ready to say goodbye to Harvey Milk. After the memorial service, people took flowers from the opera house and passed them out to strangers on the streets. Even Milk's ashes were disseminated. Friends scattered most of the ashes in San Francisco Bay, and they buried some of them beneath the sidewalk in front of Castro Camera. A plaque that covers those ashes reads:

> Harvey Milk made history as the first openly-gay elected official in California, and one of the first in the nation, when he won election to the San Francisco Board of Supervisors in November 1977. His camera store and campaign headquarters at 575 Castro Street and his apartment upstairs were centers of community activism for a wide range of human rights, environmental, labor and neighborhood issues. Harvey Milk's hard work and accomplishments on behalf of all San Franciscans earned him widespread respect and support. His life is an inspiration to all people committed to equal opportunity and an end to bigotry.
>
> You gotta give 'em hope!

Even after all the ceremonies, friends of Harvey Milk sought closure in the form of justice. Dan White, they felt, needed to be prosecuted and locked away.

The prosecution team asked for the death penalty, and most people felt that such a verdict, or at least a life term in prison, would be inevitable. After all, there was no doubt that White had committed the murders. He had walked into Moscone's office, and witnesses had heard shots. Other witnesses had seen him greet Milk, had heard the shots that killed him, and had seen him walk out of the bloody office. Moreover, White had confessed to the shootings.

The killings also seemed to be premeditated, first-degree murders. White had ventured to city hall with a loaded gun and extra bullets. He asked to see the mayor, and then shot him not just once but four times—once in the arm and three times in the head. The five shots he fired at Milk included two to the head at point-blank range. That he murdered two high-level politicians, including the mayor of one of the nation's largest cities, should have sealed his fate.

Had Moscone and Milk been part of the traditional establishment, and if White had been on the fringe of society, he likely would have been sentenced to death or life in prison. But many conservative whites viewed Moscone and Milk as enemies of everything they believed in and supported. Some even considered White to be a hero.

Most members of the San Francisco Police Department had considered Moscone too liberal and were bothered by the growing gay population. Following the murder, some police openly wore T-shirts that said "Free Dan White."

As White sat in jail awaiting trial, one law enforcement official came to a realization. "The more I observed what went on at the jail," he said, "the more I began to stop seeing what Dan White did as the act of an individual and began to see it as a political act in a political movement."

During the trial, no African Americans or Asians were selected for the jury. Most of those selected were white, working-class Catholics—just like White—and many lived close to his neighborhood. Also significant, no homosexuals were selected for the jury. Those gays who were considered were eventually disqualified. Their sexual orientation, it was thought, would make them prejudiced against White. The gay community was outraged. Wouldn't the white, Catholic heterosexuals, they argued, be prejudiced for White?

In the opening argument, defense attorney Doug Schmidt set the tone for the trial when he said: "Good people, fine people, with fine backgrounds, simply don't kill people in cold blood."

The prosecution's case against White was weak. They spent three days proving that White had killed Moscone and Milk when White had already confessed to doing so. Then, when they played an audio-tape of his confession, it backfired. Some jurors cried as a weeping White explained his motive:

> I've been under an awful lot of pressure lately—finan-cial pressure because of my job situation. Family pressure. Not being able to have time with my family. [Begins to cry.] The mayor never called me. He told me he was going to call me before he made any decision, and he never did that. It was only on my own initiative when I went down today to speak with him. I was troubled . . . . I was just going to the mayor just to see if he was going to reappoint me—just all the time knowing he's going to go out and lie to the press and tell them that I wasn't a good supervisor and that people didn't want me, and then that was it. Then I . . . I just shot him.
>
> And then it struck me about what Harvey had tried to do. And I said, well, I'll go talk to him. You know, at least maybe he'll be honest with me. And he was all smiles and stuff, and I went in . . . he knew I wasn't going to be reap-pointed. And he just kind of smirked at me, as if to say too bad. And then I just got all flushed and hot . . . and I shot him.

Besides garnering the jury's sympathy, the defense team tried to prove that the killings were not first-degree murders. Attorney Doug Schmidt subpoenaed numerous character witnesses (family members, police officers, firefighters) and psychiatrists who lauded White or made excuses for his actions. One psychiatrist said that White suffered from manic-depression. His condition was exacerbated by an unusual amount of junk food that he had recently eaten. White's mental state, the law-yers said, was one of "diminished capacity," and the salty, sugary food helped send him over the edge. Newspapers derided the claim as the "Twinkie defense."

What about White's premeditative actions? One psychiatrist testified that White brought the gun and extra bullets to city hall because it gave him a feeling of security during a time in which he felt threatened. Another psychiatrist said that White knew that his gun would cause an awkward situation with the guard at the city hall entrance. To spare the officer the feeling of embarrassment, the witness said, White entered through the window.

On May 21, 1979, the jury announced its verdict. Instead of first-degree murder, they found White guilty of voluntary manslaughter. He

Hostess Twinkies (*Courtesy of Larry D. Moore*)

was sentenced to seven years and eight months in prison. With good behavior, he could be released in five years. Upon hearing his fate, White broke into tears.

Most San Franciscans were stunned by the decision. Mayor Feinstein said she received news of the verdict "with disbelief." Said Harry Britt, who Feinstein had appointed as Milk's replacement as supervisor: "This insane jury has legitimized the immorality of this killer. Every gay will know that this man's act represented intense homophobia."

"It was a wrong decision," said District Attorney Joseph Freitas, Jr. "The jury was overwhelmed by emotions and did not sufficiently analyze the evidence that this was deliberate, calculated murder."

Less than an hour after the verdict, some 1,500 demonstrators descended on city hall. Chanting "Remember Harvey," they pushed up against the front doors and pounded the glass—breaking it—with their fists. The demonstration lasted about two hours until dozens of police officers, wielding tear gas, arrived to disperse the crowd.

The violence, though, was just beginning. Demonstrators set fires in trash cans and newspaper stands. Others smashed the windows of cars, stores, and houses. By 10 p.m., some 5,000 people had amassed near city hall. Police felt so outnumbered that they took cover in the building.

Demonstrators set fire to police cars, threw bricks at city hall windows, and hurled tear gas canisters, which they had stolen from the police cars. "Get Dan White," people shouted. "Lynch him." Reinforcements arrived to subdue the mob. In what was dubbed the White Night Riots, more than 140 people—including sixty police officers—were injured, and about two dozen demonstrators were arrested.

The following night, some 3,000 people gathered in the Castro to celebrate Harvey Milk's forty-ninth birthday. Disco music filled the air and no major incidents developed. In fact, many people wore T-shirts

Burning San Francisco police cruisers *(Courtesy Robert Clay / Alamy)*

that said, "No Violence, Please." They were ready to put the grief and anger behind them and honor their old friend in peace.

On January 6, 1984, White—just thirty-seven years old—was released from Soledad Prison. He served a year of parole time in Los Angeles, and then—against the wishes of Mayor Feinstein—returned to San Francisco. White and his wife tried to make their marriage work, but after all that had happened and in his troubled mental state, they were unable to live together.

Police officers and demonstrators are seen outside city hall during a riot that broke out following the controversial sentencing of Dan White, who was found guilty of manslaughter on May 21, 1979. *(Courtesy of AP Images)*

On October 21, 1985, Dan White entered his garage and rigged a garden hose from his car's exhaust pipe to the interior. He rolled up the windows, started the car, and waited to die. His brother found him dead later that afternoon.

Thirteen years later, on September 18, 1998, a chilling article appeared in the San Jose Mercury News. Frank Falzon, who had been a friend of White while working at the San Francisco Police Department, revealed to reporter Mike Weiss what White had told him in 1984.

"I really lost it that day," White said, according to Falzon. "I was on a mission. I wanted four of them." According to this alleged confession, White planned to kill Moscone, Milk, a woman on the Board of Supervisors, and an African American state assemblyman who was Moscone's close ally.

"Carol Ruth Silver," White said, "she was the biggest snake . . . and Willie Brown, he was masterminding the whole thing." Falzon firmly believed White's confession. "I felt like I had been hit by a sledge-hammer," Falzon said. "I found out it was a premeditated murder."

In 1998, Brown recalled that he had left Moscone's office just moments before White entered it. "[White] missed me by 30 seconds," said Brown, who went on to serve as San Francisco's mayor from 1996 to 2004. If White hadn't killed Moscone and Milk, Brown said, "the city would have been a far more liberal and progressive place than it currently is."

8

MILK'S LEGACY

If Harvey Milk were still alive today—which is certainly plausible since he was born in 1930—he would delight in the story told by his nephew. Twenty-five years after Milk's assassination, Stuart Milk traveled to California to speak at the University of San Francisco. Milk always had been supportive of the elderly, and so was Stuart, who helped an old woman carry her groceries. The woman asked the man for his name.

"I'm Stuart Milk," he said.

"Are you any relation to Harvey Milk?" she asked.

"I'm his nephew," he said.

"You know," she said, "your uncle changed my thinking. He opened my mind. He changed the way I viewed life."

Milk had that effect on people. And that is one reason that he is hailed as a hero—a martyr, an icon, a legend—more than thirty years after his death.

At the turn of the century, *Time* magazine unveiled "The Time 100: The Most Important People of the Century." A subcategory was "Heroes and Icons: Twenty people who articulate the longings of the last 100 years, exemplifying courage, selflessness, exuberance, superhuman ability and amazing grace." This group of extraordinary individuals included Anne Frank, Billy Graham, Helen Keller, Muhammad Ali, the Kennedys, Rosa Parks, Jackie Robinson, Mother Teresa, and Harvey Milk.

Milk, wrote *Time* writer John Cloud, "became the first openly gay man elected to any substantial political office in the history of the planet." Yet many other reasons explain

Harvey Milk in 1978, San Francisco, California

(Courtesy of Robert Clay / Alamy)

why Milk is, in immortality, as highly esteemed as Mother Teresa and the Kennedys.

In the U.S. city with the largest per-capita homosexual population, Milk pushed through the strongest gay-rights legislation yet scene in America. Then, like a Hall of Fame quarterback, he orchestrated a tremendous grassroots comeback to defeat Proposition 6—turning a potentially disastrous defeat into a rousing victory.

After winning election as supervisor, he made good on his promise to support more than just his gay constituents. Milk supported the rights of Asians, African Americans, the disabled, senior citizens—any group that traditionally had gotten the short end of the stick. Said Dianne Feinstein, "His homosexuality gave him an insight into the scars which all oppressed people wear. He believed that no sacrifice was too great a price to pay for the cause of human rights."

As San Francisco's gay population grew exponentially in the 1970s, Milk filled the leadership vacuum. Other local gay politicians took cautious steps, but Milk made loud vocal demands. Under threat of assassination during the 1978 Gay Freedom Day Parade, Milk penned the following words to his speech: "Jimmy Carter . . . it is up to you. And now, before it becomes too late, come to California and speak out against Briggs. If you don't, then we will come to you!" To fellow gays, he stated in the speech: "If Briggs wins . . . there will be no safe 'closet' for any gay person. So break out of yours today—tear the damn thing down once and for all!"

It is easy to see why homosexuals, who could be hauled off and beaten by police just for walking down the sidewalk, hailed the man who repeatedly went to bat for them. Milk's demeanor also added to his legend. While lamenting that Milk's political career had ended so soon, John Cloud wrote in *Time*: "His politics-as-theater and his humor would have been a tonic for the seriousness that often grips gay politics, driving young people away from it."

Milk was deathly serious when he needed to be, but he also charmed people young and old with his enthusiasm, humor, and seize-the-day philosophy. A day before his forty-eighth (and last) birthday, Milk

Harvey Milk in a promo for Ringling Brothers Barnum & Bailey's Circus. Six local celebrities were invited to dress up as clowns for a day. *(Courtesy of Dan Nicoletta)*

dressed up as a clown as a publicity stunt for Barnum & Bailey's circus. He was in his glory, for he loved to clown around.

Perhaps Milk's greatest impact—and he realized it too—was the inspiration and hope he provided to thousands of young homosexuals. Dustin Lance Black was one such individual. As an adolescent in the 1980s, Black moved with his family from a conservative Mormon home in San Antonio, Texas, to California. It was there that he first heard the recordings of Harvey Milk.

"I was listening to one of his speeches right after he was elected to public office," Black said, "and he says something like, 'There's a kid out there, maybe in San Antonio, who's going to hear my story and hear that an openly gay man was elected to public office—and it's going to give him hope.' And I just lost it because that's exactly what it did for me."

Some historians have compared Milk to Martin Luther King, Jr., and the comparison is not farfetched. Born just a year apart, both men were intelligent and perceptive. Each emerged as a leader of a burgeoning movement, largely because of their exceptional abilities but also because of happenstance. King was a minister in Montgomery, Alabama, in 1955 when Rosa Parks' defiance triggered the bus boycott—the springboard for the civil rights movement. Milk happened to be running for public office in San Francisco during the emergence of the gay-rights movement.

Both Milk and King were charismatic individuals with crossover appeal, and each was a powerful speaker who brought crowds to their feet. Both were assassinated in the prime of life—King in 1968 and Milk ten years later. Their status as martyrs has inspired others to pick up the torch and fight for equal rights.

Many of Milk's supporters went on to devote their lives to helping others and furthering the cause for homosexuals. Harry Britt and Cleve Jones are two bright lights. Britt, a friend of Milk who replaced him as supervisor, eventually became president of the board and introduced domestic partner (similar to gay marriage) legislation to San Francisco. Jones, another close friend of Milk, co-founded the San Francisco AIDS Foundation. In 1985, while at a memorial for Milk, he conceived the idea of the AIDS Memorial Quilt. The quilt, which grew to become the world's largest community arts project, is an extraordinary tribute to those who have died of AIDS.

Directly and indirectly, Milk changed laws and politics. In 1982, the "diminished capacity" defense, used most famously in the Dan White trial, was abolished in California. Milk also broke down barriers for gay politicians. Today, more than 150 openly gay men and lesbians have been elected to public office in almost every state in the country. Massachusetts democrat Barney Frank, a gay man, became a U.S. representative in 1981 and has gone on to become one of the most powerful congressmen on Capitol Hill.

Many have wondered what impact Milk would have had in dealing with the HIV/AIDS epidemic, which emerged in the early 1980s. Thousands of gay men contracted the deadly disease, largely through unprotected sex. What role would Milk have played during the ordeal?

Over the last quarter-century, activists have struggled to raise awareness, and sufficient funding, for HIV/AIDS. Would Milk's clout have made a stronger impact? And would he have worked within the system or joined ACT UP, which has staged aggressive demonstrations on behalf of AIDS patience? One thing is for sure, said California assemblyman Tom Ammiano: "He was an activist at heart. He would have been very aggressive in fighting AIDS from day one."

Over the years, Milk's supporters and admirers have worked to preserve his legacy. The Harvey Milk Gay Democratic Club is now the Harvey Milk Lesbian, Gay, Bisexual, Transgender Democratic Club. Nicknamed the Milk Club, the organization boasts of "pushing issues that have changed the world," including "early explicit sex education about HIV and inventing the idea of domestic partnerships."

The Harvey Milk Civil Rights Academy, founded in the Castro district in 1996, is an alternative elementary school. The school stresses tolerance, nonviolence, diversity, academic excellence, and community involvement—issues that Milk strongly believed in.

The San Francisco library system has a Harvey Milk Memorial Branch in Eureka Valley. At the University of Texas at Austin, the

Lyndon Baines Johnson School of Public Affairs includes the Harvey Milk Society, which provides support for lesbian, gay, bisexuals, and transgender (LGBT) individuals.

In San Francisco, numerous memorials honor the fallen hero. The former site of Castro Camera—Milk's business and campaign head-quarters—was designated a historic building. Moreover, a historic San Francisco streetcar was dedicated to the memory of Milk. On Milk's birthday in 2006, a permanent photographic tribute was unveiled at Harvey Milk Plaza, which is located at Market and Castro Streets. In celebration of his birthday two years later, a bust of Milk was unveiled at city hall, outside the supervisors' meeting room.

Two men look at a streetcar dedicated to former San Francisco supervisor Harvey Milk in San Francisco, October 28, 2008. The San Francisco Municipal Transportation Authority dedicated a historic Municipal Railway streetcar to the memory of Milk. *(Courtesy of AP Images)*

Every medium imaginable has been used to recreate Milk's dramatic career. *The Times of Harvey Milk*, an emotionally powerful film, won an Academy Award for best documentary of 1984. *The Harvey Milk Show*, a musical theater production, premiered in 1991, and an opera entitled *Harvey Milk* opened to mixed reviews in 1996.

The fun-loving Milk would have been first in line for these shows, but he likely would have been most proud of Harvey Milk High School, which was established in 1985 in the East Village of New York City. Studies have shown that LGBT (lesbian, gay, bisexual and transgender) teenagers are bullied more than heterosexual students and are more prone to drug use, depression, and thoughts of suicide. Harvey Milk High, with an enrollment of more than a hundred, provides a safe and supportive environment for LGBT students. It also boasts of a graduation rate that exceeds 90 percent—well above average for a New York City school.

In 2008 and '09, Harvey Milk entered the consciousness of a new generation of Americans. During the summer and fall, Proposition 8 was the topic of conversations throughout California. Opponents of gay marriage (which in mid-2008 was legal only in Massachusetts and California) started an initiative to outlaw the practice in California. In November, Proposition 8—which asked whether same-sex couples should have the right to get married in California—went on the ballot in the Golden State.

Even if Prop 8 were defeated, gay couples still would have been protected by domestic partnership rights. These rights guarantee most of the legal rights of marriage; for example, if only one member is working, the nonworking partner can be covered on the working partner's health insurance plan. However, married couples have a few more rights than domestic partners; for example, domestic partners must share a residence or risk losing certain benefits, while married couples do not need to live together to receive such benefits. Perhaps more importantly, being told that they cannot be married is a devastating emotional blow to many gay and lesbian couples.

Proposition 8 was hugely contentious. Those for and against the initiative raised approximately $40 million each to fight the other side. Along the way, numerous pundits compared Prop 8 to the Prop 6 battle that Milk had led thirty years earlier. Wrote Jess McKinley in the *New York Times*: "Call it life imitating 'Milk,' or vice versa, but the parallels between the [1978] campaign . . . and the real-life battle over Proposition 8 are striking. Social conservatives pitted against gay activists? Check. A Republican governor (and former movie star) siding with gay Californians [Ronald Reagan and Arnold Schwarzenegger]? Check. Close polls, a nationally watched campaign, the potential for heartbreak? Check, check, check."

This time, however, the outcome was different. Prop 8 passed by a vote of 52.3 percent to 47.7 percent. Homosexuals could no longer get married in California. The vote was so close that one has to wonder: would

Michele and Elizabeth Ochoa watch a "No on Prop 8" rally on Sunday, November 2, 2008, in Fresno, California. *(Courtesy of AP Images)*

the result have been different if a leader as dynamic as Harvey Milk had been involved?

Perhaps Prop 8 would have been defeated if the film *Milk* had been released earlier in the year. The movie premiered in San Francisco on October 28, 2008 (seven days before the vote), and it opened nationwide in late November. *Milk* is a rousing biopic about Milk's glory years in San Francisco. His fight against Prop 6 and his stirring messages of hope are central to the story.

Millions of moviegoers were inspired by Harvey Milk's story and became sympathetic to the cause of gay rights. Critics, meanwhile, hailed the film as powerful, poignant, and historically accurate. *Milk* was honored with two Academy Awards—one for Sean Penn (who played Milk) for best actor and the other for Dustin Lance Black for best original screenplay.

On Oscar night, an emotional Black concluded his acceptance speech with a reference to Prop 8 and a tribute to his idol. "If Harvey had not been taken from us thirty years ago," Black said, "I think he'd want me to say to all of the gay and lesbian kids out there tonight who have been told that they are 'less than' by their churches, by the government, or by their families, that you are beautiful, wonderful creatures of value. And that no matter what anyone tells you, God does love you and that very soon, I promise you, you will have equal rights, federally, across this great nation of ours."

"Thank you," Black said amid thunderous applause. "Thank you. And thank you, God, for giving us Harvey Milk."

In August 2009, President Barack Obama bestowed the nation's highest civilian honor on the slain San Francisco supervisor, making Milk the first openly gay civil rights leader to receive the Presidential Medal of Freedom. Stuart Milk, Harvey Milk's nephew, accepted the medal on the family's behalf.

"In the prime of his life, he was silenced by the act of another," President Obama said. "But in the brief time in which he spoke, and ran and led, his voice stirred the aspirations of millions of people. . . . And his message of hope—hope unashamed, hope unafraid—could not ever be silenced. It was Harvey who said it best: 'You gotta give 'em hope.'"

Stuart Milk, nephew of slain San Francisco supervisor Harvey Milk, accepts the 2009 Presidential Medal of Freedom for his uncle from President Barack Obama, right, at the White House in Washington, August 12, 2009. *(Courtesy of AP Images)*

TIMELINE

1930: Born on May 22 in Woodmere, New York.

1947: Graduated from Bayshore High School; arrested for congregating with homosexuals in New York's Central Park.

1951: Graduates from the New York State College for Teachers.

1951-55: Serves in the Navy, achieving the rank of lieutenant, junior grade.

1956-72: Works at multiple jobs, including teacher, actuarial statistician, investment researcher, and theatrical producer; lives in New York City and, for brief periods, in Dallas and San Francisco.

1973: Opens Castro Camera in the Castro district of San Francisco with partner Scott Smith; fails in his first attempt to win election to the San Francisco Board of Supervisors.

1974: Establishes the Castro Village Association, comprised of local gay business owners.

1975: Fails in his second attempt to win election to the San Francisco Board of Supervisors.

1976: Sworn in as a member of the San Francisco Board of Permit Appeals, after being appointed by Mayor George Moscone; fired five weeks later after insisting on running for a seat in the California State Assembly; loses in his attempt to win a seat in the California State Assembly.

1977: Leads a march through San Francisco in protest over the repeal of gay-rights legislation in Dade County, Florida; announces his candidacy for city supervisor.

1978: Achieves his greatest success as a legislator when the Board of Supervisors passes a strong gay-rights ordinance in San Francisco; leads effort to defeat the Briggs Initiative (Proposition 6); celebrates the defeat of Proposition 6; fatally shot and killed on November 27 by Dan White.

1979: Jury finds Dan White guilty of voluntary manslaughter, and sentences him to seven years and eight months in prison; outraged, gays and other protesters riot in San Francisco.

1985: *The Times of Harvey Milk* wins an Academy Award for best documentary film; the Harvey Milk High School for LGBT students founded in New York City.

2009: *Milk*, a film starring actor Sean Penn as Harvey Milk, wins two Academy Awards; President Barack Obama awards Milk the Presidential Medal of Freedom.

SOURCES

CHAPTER ONE: Wake Up, America

p. 7, "You get the . . . " Randy Shilts, *The Mayor of Castro Street* (New York: St. Martin's Press, 1982), 223.

p. 7, "Christian beliefs regarding . . ." Mark Silk and Andrew Walsh, *One Nation, Divisible* (Lanham, Md.: Rowman & Littlefield, 2008), 71.

p. 8-10, "My name is . . . leave it," Shilts, *The Mayor of Castro Street*, 224-25.

CHAPTER TWO: Harvey's Secret

p. 17, "He was funny . . ." Carol Polsky, "Hidden depths of Long Island native Harvey Milk," *Newsday,* January 11, 2009,

p. 18, "I think that . . ." Ibid.

p. 19, "And they say . . ." Ibid.

p. 23, "warm, lovable guy . . ." Polsky, "Hidden depths of Long Island native Harvey Milk," *Newsday,* January 11, 2009.

p. 23, "I was just . . ." Ibid.

p. 25, "How could you not . . .

CHAPTER THREE: Winds of Change

p. 29, "Gold! Gold! Gold . . ." "California Geological Survey—Gold," State of California Department of Conservation, 2007, http://www.conservation.ca.gov/cgs/geologic_resources/gold/Pages/index.aspx.

p. 30, "A knock at . . .," John Gruen, "'Do You Mind Critics Calling You Cheap, Decadent Sensationalistic, Gimmicky, Vulgar, Overinflated, Megalomaniacal?'" *New York Times Magazine,* January 2, 1972.

p. 36, "We do not . . ." Shilts, *The Mayor of Castro Street,* 64.

p. 36, "Harvey spent most . . ." Ann Walton Sieber, "Harvey Milk," *OutSmart,* http://www.outsmartmagazine.com/issue/i05-00/milk.html.

CHAPTER FOUR: The Mayor of Castro Street

p. 39, "You mean I . . ." Shilts, *The Mayor of Castro Street,* 71.

p. 40, "get involved and . . ." Ibid., 72.

p. 42, "a crumb thrown . . ." Shilts, *The Mayor of Castro Street,* 80.

p. 43, "You could see . . ." Ron Williams, "I Remember Harvey," WebCastro, 1995, http://www.webcastro.com/harvey.htm.

p. 44, "I have tasted . . ." Jesse Hamlin, "Quotes from Harvey Milk and friends," SFGate, November 23, 2008, http://www.sfgate.com/cgi-bin/article.cgi?f=/c/a/2008/11/21/PKBJ13VKO5.DTL&type=gaylesbian.

p. 45, "Lo and behold . . ." Rob Epstein, *The Times of Harvey Milk* (Black Sand Productions, 1984), documentary.

p. 45, "You've got to. . . " Hamlin, "Quotes from Harvey Milk and friends," SFGate.

p. 47, "pigs . . ." Shilts, *The Mayor of Castro Street,* 92.

p. 51, "It's too good . . ." Ibid., 122.

p. 51, "screwed up mentally . . ." Associated Press, Stephen Fox, "I'm no hero,' man who saved Ford says," *Wisconsin State Journal,* September 24, 1975.

p. 52, "He opened the . . ." Carl Nolte, "City Hall Slayings: 25 Years Later," *San Francisco Chronicle,* November 26, 2003, http://www.sfgate.com/cgi-bin/article.cgi?file=/c/a/2003/11/26/MNGF33B0R31.DTL.

CHAPTER FIVE: Milk vs. The Machine

p. 56, "I think a . . ." Shilts, *The Mayor of Castro Street,* 134.

p. 57, "Make sure you're . . ." Ibid., 139.

p. 58, "No decisions which . . ." Ibid., 150.

p. 59, "What these people . . ." Ashley Fantz, "Queer Adoption," *Miami New Times,* May 23, 2002, www.miaminewtimes.com/2002-05-23/news/queer-adoption/5.

p. 59, "As a mother . . ." "Queerly Spoken," Lesbian News, http://www.thelnmag.com/quote.html.

p. 61, "All America and . . ." B. Drummond Ayers, Jr., "Miami Votes 2 to 1 to Repeal Law Barring Bias Against Homosexuals," *New York Times,* June 8, 1977.

p. 61, "This is the . . ." David Eisenbach, *Gay Power* (New York: Carroll and Graf Publishers, 2006), 286.

p. 62, "faggot, faggot, faggot . . ." Shilts, The Mayor of Castro Street, 163.

p. 63, "[I]t's not my . . ." Ibid., 165.

CHAPTER SIX: The Historic Election

p. 65, "That campaign was . . ." Epstein, *The Times of Harvey Milk.*

p. 65, "I looked at . . ." Ibid.

p. 66, "He was a . . ." Ibid.

p. 66, "we don't want . . ." John Patterson, "If I'm killed, let that bullet destroy every closet door," *The Guardian,* December 6, 2008, http://www.guardian.co.uk/film/2008/dec/06/harvey-milk?loc=interstitialskip.

p. 67, "The victory will . . ." United Press International, "Homosexual Wins in SF," (San Mateo) *Times,* November 9, 1977.

p. 67, "and I'll be . . ." Ibid.

p. 70, "This is similar . . ." Ibid.

p. 70, "If he had . . ." "Another Day of Death," *Time,* December 11, 1978, http://www.time.com/time/magazine/article/0,9171,919893,00.html.

p. 70, "Dan White is . . ." Shilts, *The Mayor of Castro Street,* 185.

p. 70, "As the years . . ." Ibid.

p. 73, "basically a decent . . ." Shilts, *The Mayor of Castro Street,* p. 197.

p. 73, "The young gay . . ." Ibid., 363.

p. 74, "This one has . . ." Les Ledbetter, "Bill on Homosexual Rights Advances in San Francisco," *New York Times,* March 22, 1978.

p. 74, "I respect the . . ." Ibid.

p. 74, "Don't knock it . . ." Shilts, *The Mayor of Castro Street,* 200.

p. 74, "Dan White was . . ." Ibid.

p. 74, "All over the . . ." Ramon Johnson, "The Harvey Milk Assassination," About.com, http://gaylife.about.com/od/gaycelebrityprofiles/p/harveymilkmilch.htm.

p. 75, "You've always loved . . ." Shilts, *The Mayor of Castro Street,* 233.

p. 76, "What Proposition 6 . . ." Epstein, *The Times of Harvey Milk.*

p. 76, "There are already . . ." Ibid.

p. 77, "I was born . . ." Ibid.

p. 77-80, "Milk: You yourself . . . oh, Senator!" Ibid.

p. 80, "Join me in . . ." Ibid.

p. 80, "Whatever else it . . ." Carl Matthes, "Milk: The Movie," LA Progressive, December 4, 2008, http://www.laprogressive.com/2008/12/04/milk-the-movie.

p. 81, "[Former president Gerald] . . ." Epstein, *The Times of Harvey Milk*.

p. 81, "Also, I want . . ." Ibid.

p. 82, "We were elated . . ." Paul VanDecarr, "Death of Dreams," *The Advocate*, Nov. 25, 2003.

p. 82, "So far, a . . ." Rob Epstein, "What Harvey Milk Tells Us About Proposition 8," November 21, 2008, *TWIT Magazine*, http://www.thisweekintexas.com/arman2/publish/CommentaryPolitics/What_Harvey Milk_Tells_Us_About_Proposition_8.php.

p. 83, "You could just . . ." Neda Ulaby, "'Gotta Give 'Em Hope': The Legacy Of Harvey Milk," NPR, 2009, http://www.npr.org/templates/story/story.php?storyId=96865519.

p. 83, "If a bullet . . ." CBS News, *People of the Century: One Hundred Men and Woman Who Shaped the Last One Hundred Years* (New York: Simon & Schuster, 1999), 365.

p. 83, " [T]hose people never . . ." Shilts, *The Mayor of Castro Street*, 373.

p. 83, "an evil man . . ." Ibid., 375.

p. 83, "playing gymnastics with . . ." Ibid., 374.

p. 83, "It's not about . . ." Ibid., 375.

CHAPTER SEVEN: Killed in Cold Blood

p. 85, "really sorry to . . ." "Another Day of Death," *Time*, December 11, 1978.

p. 88, "Rev. Jones is . . ." Harvey Milk, letter to President Jimmy Carter, February 19, 1978, http://www.brasscheck.com/jonestown/milk.jpg.

p. 88, "I proceeded to . . ." "Another Day of Death," *Time*.

p. 90, "I was worried . . .," Ibid.

p. 90, "It was awful. . ." Nolte, "City Hall Slayings: 25 Years Later," *San Francisco Chronicle*.

p. 90, "Harvey, can I . . ." "Another Day of Death," *Time*.

p. 91, "Oh, no . . ." Shilts, *The Mayor of Castro Street*, 269.

p. 91, "I put my . . ." Nolte, "City Hall Slayings: 25 Years Later," *San Francisco Chronicle*.

p. 91, "He was a . . ." "Another Day of Death," *Time*.

p. 92, "As president of . . ." Jerry Roberts, *Dianne Feinstein: Never Let Them See You Cry* (New York: HarperCollinsWest, 1994), 172.

p. 92, "hard-working and dedicated . . ." Hamlin, "Quotes from Harvey Milk and friends," SFGate.

p. 92, "Are you happy . . ." "Another Day of Death," *Time*.

p. 96, "The murders of . . ." Shilts, *The Mayor of Castro Street*, 284.

p. 96, "I can be . . ." Uncle Donald's Castro Street, Jan. 22, 2002, http://thecastro.net/milk/memorial.html.

p. 97, "He knew that. . ." Ibid.

p. 98, "Harvey Milk made . . ." *San Francisco Sentinel*, http://www.sanfranciscosentinel.com/wp-content uploads/2007/05/harvey-milk-2-photo-sho.jpg.

p. 99, "The more I . . ." Warren Hinckle, *Gayslayer! The Story of How Dan White Killed Harvey Milk and George Moscone & Got Away with Murder* (Virginia City, Nevada: Silver Dollar Books, 1985).

p. 99, "Good people, fine . . ." Gary David Comstock, *Violence Against Lesbians and Gay Men* (New York: Columbia University Press, 1995), 88.

p. 100, "I've been under . . ." Epstein, *The Times of Harvey Milk*.

p. 101, "with disbelief . . ." Wallace Turner, "Ex-Official Guilty of Manslaughter In Slayings on Coast; 3,000 Protest," *New York Times*, May 22, 1979.

p. 101, "This insane jury . . ." Ibid.

p. 102, "It was a . . ." Ibid.

p. 102, "Remember Harvey . . ." Ibid.

p. 104, "Get Dan White . . ." Les Ledbetter, "San Francisco Tense as Violence Follows Murder Trial," *New York Times,* May 23, 1979.

p. 105, "I really lost . . ." Mike Weiss, "Killer of Moscone, Milk Had Willie Brown on List," *San Jose Mercury News,* September 18, 1998.

p. 105, "Carol Ruth Silver . . ." Ibid.

p. 105, "I felt like . . ." Ibid.

p. 105, "[White] missed me . . ." Ibid.

CHAPTER EIGHT: Harvey's Legacy

p. 107, "I'm Stuart Milk . . ." Nolte, "City Hall Slayings: 25 Years Later," *San Francisco Chronicle.*

p. 107, "Heroes and Icons . . ." "Heroes and Icons," *Time,* http://www.time.com/time/time100/heroes.

p. 108, "became the first . . ." John Cloud, "Harvey Milk, *Time,* June 14, 1999, http://www.time.com/time/time100/heroes/profile/milk01.html.

p. 108, "His homosexuality gave . . ." "40 Heroes," Advocate.com, http://www.advocate.com/issue_story_ektid48675.asp?page=2.

p. 108, "Jimmy Carter . . ." Shilts, *The Mayor of Castro Street,* 369-70.

p. 108, "If Briggs wins. . ." Ibid., 368.

p. 109, "His politics-as-theater and . . ." John Cloud, "Why Milk Is Still Fresh," The Free Library, 1998, http://www.thefreelibrary.com/Why+Milk+is+still+fresh. (Harvey+Milk)-a054879376.

p. 110, "I was listening . . ." Kyle Buchanan, "The Gay M.L.K.," *Advocate,* February 26, 2008.

p. 111, "He was an . . ." Chris Bull, "Continuing Milk's Legacy, *Advocate,* November 11, 2003.

p. 111, "pushing issues that . . ." "Join the Milk Club," Milk Club, http://www.milkclub.org.

p. 115, "Call it life . . ." Jess McKinley, "Back to the Ramparts in California," *New York Times,* November 1, 2008.

p. 116, "If Harvey had . . ." Roger Goodman and Allen P. Haines, *The 81st Annual Academy Awards, WLS-Chicago, February 22, 2009.*

p. 116, "In the prime . . ." Lou Chibbaro Jr., "Milk's Family Reflects on Medal of Freedom Honor," Washingtonblade.com, August 21, 2009, http://www.washblade.com/2009/8-21/news/national/15060.cfm.

BIBLIOGRAPHY

Alsenas, Linas. *Gay America: Struggle for Equality.* New York: Amulet, 2008.

"Another Day of Death." *Time,* December 11, 1978.

Ayers, B. Drummond, Jr. "Miami Votes 2 to 1 to Repeal Law Barring Bias Against Homosexuals." *New York Times,* June 8, 1977.

Buchanan, Kyle. "The Gay M.L.K." *Advocate,* February 26, 2008.

Bull, Chris. "Continuing Milk's Legacy." *Advocate,* November 11, 2003.

Carter, David. *Stonewall: The Riots That Sparked the Gay Revolution.* New York: Macmillan, 2004.

CBS News. *People of the Century: One Hundred Men and Woman Who Shaped the Last One Hundred Years.* New York: Simon & Schuster, 1999.

Cloud, John. "Harvey Milk." *Time,* June 14, 1999, http://www.time.com/time/time100/heroes/profile/milk01.html.

———. "Why Milk Is Still Fresh." The Free Library, 1998, http://www.thefreelibrary.com/Why+Milk+is+still+fresh.(Harvey+Milk)-a054879376.

Comstock, Gary David. *Violence Against Lesbians and Gay Men.* New York: Columbia University Press, 1995.

De Jim, Strange. *San Francisco's Castro.* Charleston, S.C.: Arcadia, 2003.

Eisenbach, David. *Gay Power.* New York: Carroll and Graf Publishers, 2006.

Epstein, Rob, director. *The Times of Harvey Milk.* Black Sand Productions, 1984.

———. "What Harvey Milk Tells Us About Proposition 8." *TWIT Magazine,* November 21, 2008, http://www.thisweekintexas.com/artman2/publish/CommentaryPolitics/What_Harvey_Milk_Tells_Us_About_Proposition_8.php.

Fantz, Ashley. "Queer Adoption." *Miami New Times,* May 23, 2002, www.miaminewtimes.com/2002-05-23/news/queer-adoption/5.

"40 Heroes." Advocate.com, http://www.advocate.com/issue_story_ektid48675.asp?page=2.

Fox, Stephen, Associated Press. "'I'm no hero,' man who saved Ford says." *Wisconsin State Journal,* September 24, 1975.

Garden, Nancy. *Hear Us Out!: Lesbian and Gay Stories of Struggle, Progress, and Hope, 1950 to the Present.* New York: Farrar, Straus and Giroux, 2007.

Goodman, Roger, and Allen P. Haines, directors. *The 81st Annual Academy Awards.* WLS-Chicago, February 22, 2009.

Gruen, John. "'Do You Mind Critics Calling You Cheap, Decadent, Sensationalistic, Gimmicky, Vulgar, Overinflated, Megalomaniacal?'" *New York Times Magazine,* January 2, 1972, http://www.orlok.com/hair/holding/articles/HairArticles/NYTMag1-2-72.html.

Herek, Gregory M. "Facts About Homosexuality and Child Molestation." UC Davis Psychology, http://psychology.ucdavis.edu/rainbow/html/facts_molestation.html.

"Heroes and Icons." *Time,* http://www.time.com/time/time100/heroes.

Hinckle, Warren. *Gayslayer! The Story of How Dan White Killed Harvey Milk and George Moscone & Got Away with Murder.* Virginia City, NV.: Silver Dollar Books, 1985.

Johnson, Ramon. "The Harvey Milk Assassination." About.com, http://gaylife.about.com/od/gaycelebrityprofiles/p/harveymilkmilch.htm.

"Join the Milk Club." Milk Club, http://www.milkclub.org.

Lamble, David. "The Boyfriend Who Nobody Understood." Diego Luna Loco, November 6, 2008, http://www.diegolunaloco.com/Press_boyfriend_nobody_understood.htm.

Ledbetter, Les. "Bill on Homosexual Rights Advances in San Francisco." *New York Times,* March 22, 1978.

———. "San Francisco Tense as Violence Follows Murder Trial." New York Times, May 23, 1979.

Lipsky, William. *Gay and Lesbian San Francisco.* Charleston, S.C.: Arcadia, 2006.

Marcus, Eric. *Making Gay History: The Half Century Fight for Lesbian and Gay Equal Rights.* New York: Harper Paperbacks, 2002.

Matthes, Carl. "Milk: The Movie." *LA Progressive,* December 4, 2008, http://www.laprogressive.com/2008/12/04/milk-the-movie.

Maupin, Armistead. "Gus Van Sant." *Interview,* December 2008.

McKinley, Jess. "Back to the Ramparts in California." *New York Times,* November 1, 2008.

Milk: A Pictorial History of Harvey Milk, with an introduction by Dustin Lance Black and foreword by Armistead Maupin. New York: Newmarket, 2009.

Milk, Harvey. Letter to President Jimmy Carter, February 19, 1978, http://www.brasscheck.com/jonestown/milk.jpg.

Nolte, Carl. "City Hall Slayings: 25 Years Later." *San Francisco Chronicle,* November 26, 2003.

Patterson, John. "If I'm killed, let that bullet destroy every closet door." *Guardian,* December 6, 2008, http://www.guardian.co.uk/film/2008/dec/06/harvey-milk?loc=interstitialskip.

Polsky, Carol. "Hidden depths of Long Island native Harvey Milk." *Newsday,* January 11, 2009, http://mobile.newsday.com/inf/infomo?view=south_suffolk_item&feed:a=newsday_5min&feed:c=southsuffolk&feed:i=44461954&nopaging=1.

"Queerly Spoken." *Lesbian News,* http://www.thelnmag.com/quote.html.

Roberts, Jerry. *Dianne Feinstein: Never Let Them See You Cry.* New York: HarperCollinsWest, 1994.

Shilts, Randy. *And the Band Played On: Politics, People, and the AIDS Epidemic.* New York: St. Martin's, 2007.

———. *The Mayor of Castro Street.* New York: St. Martin's, 1982.

Sieber, Ann Walton. "Harvey Milk." OutSmart, http://www.outsmartmagazine.com/issue/i05-00/milk.html.

Silk, Mark, and Andrew Walsh. *One Nation, Divisible.* Lanham, Md.: Rowman & Littlefield, 2008.

State of California Department of Conservation, 2007, http://www.conservation.ca.gov/cgs/geologic_resources/gold/Pages/index.aspx.

Taylor, Michael. "Jones Captivated S.F.'s Liberal Elite." SFGate, November 12, 1998, http://www.sfgate.com/cgi-bin/article.cgi?file=/chronicle/archive/1998/11/12/MN85578.DTL.

Turner, Wallace. "Ex-Official Guilty of Manslaughter In Slayings on Coast; 3,000 Protest." *New York Times,* May 22, 1979.

Ulaby, Neda. "'Gotta Give 'Em Hope': The Legacy Of Harvey Milk." NPR, 2009, http://www.npr.org/templates/story/story.php?storyId=96865519.

Uncle Donald's official Web site. "The Mayor of Castro Street." http://thecastro.net/milk/memorial.html.

United Press International. "Homosexual Wins in SF." (San Mateo) *Times,* November 9, 1977.

VanDecarr, Paul. "Death of Dreams." *Advocate,* November 25, 2003.

Weiss, Mike. "Killer of Moscone, Milk Had Willie Brown on List." *San Jose Mercury News,* September 18, 1998.

Williams, Ron. "I Remember Harvey." WebCastro, 1995, http://www.webcastro.com/harvey.htm.

WEB SITES

http://www.time.com/time/time100/heroes/profile/milk01.html
In 1999, *Time* magazine named Harvey Milk one of the "100 Most Important People of the Century," and visitors to this site can learn why by reading an article by *Time* correspondent John Cloud.

http://topics.nytimes.com/top/reference/timestopics/people/m/harvey_ milk/index.html?inline=nyt-per
A biography of Harvey Milk, along with links to a long list of articles and even audio and video clips, is featured on this *New York Times* online site.

http://thecastro.net/milkpage.html
The personal Website of "Uncle Donald" provides links to a full range of articles and images of Milk.

http://www.glbtq.com/social-sciences/milk_h.html
GLBTQ, an online encyclopedia of gay, lesbian, bisexual, transgender, and queer culture, features a three-page biography of Milk's life and legacy.

INDEX